Sport Is War

Sport Is War

WRITTEN BY MICHAEL A. ROSEL

Table of Contents

Foreword

IN A HOTEL room somewhere in the mid-west, the major brain trust of a National League baseball team gather to plot a strategy designed to win the pennant, and put their team in the World Series. Down south, in another hotel, management from an American League team is pursuing the same agenda. The people query their scouts, and they consult books filled with statistical analysis. Both groups have a copy of "Money Ball", the book that redefined baseball analysis, lying nearby. Someone opens up a lap top and begins to show the others video highlights of different prospective baseball players' talents.

"Watch the footwork of this shortstop, gentlemen."

"Wow! What an arm that right fielder has. Where did he go to school?"

The discussions and the analysis go on well into the night. From 1869 and the first professional baseball team, the Cincinnati Red Stockings, people have tried to get an advantage over their opponents. Men and women compete in this world for resources, power, money, and prestige. When I say men are competitive, I mean mankind is competitive. But when it comes to recreational sporting endeavors, predominantly, it is the male of the species that obsesses over the box score.

Some years ago, I saw a magazine cover. It read: the American League Arms Race. They weren't talking about the nuclear arms race or gravitas. It (the magazine cover) pictured baseball players sporting rifles, AK-47's, and sub-machine guns -- in place of their arms. The Kansas City Royals had just signed Mark Davis. He was a relief pitcher. Davis had been awarded the coveted Cy Young Award in 1989. The Royals already had a starter named Bret Saberhagen, who had previously won the Cy Young Award. I reasoned they were sure to win the pennant that year. I wagered $100, with 3 to 1 odds, in Reno over the winter; based, primarily, on this information, along with this magazine article - praising the Royals' arms. Well, the Royals didn't win the pennant.

The passion we exude as we follow our teams through their trials and tribulations, the countless hours of studying saber metrics, the research, the calculations, and the wagering - all lead me to this one conclusion: That sport Is war.

(1)

Knights in White Satin

MOST WARS THAT have been fought by mankind have had little or no moral high-ground. Wars have been fought for conquest. Most of the time wars are fought because of a ruler's vanity. In this world seldom is there a clear case of good vs.: evil where a white knight faces off against a black knight.

Occasionally armies are raised to save a people from an oppressor. Sometimes tremendous moral imperatives are at stake. Churchill vs. Hitler could be categorized this way. Halsey vs. Yamamoto at Midway was white vs. black. George G. Meade vs. Robert E. Lee is another example where the fate of our union was at stake. But these so called just wars are few and far between. The Great War was a war to end all wars and to make the world safe for democracy. It, the First World War, was such a big hit it required a sequel. But all jesting aside, what Tom Brokaw calls the greatest generation *did* save the world from Nazi Germany and Imperial Japan. The Russians suffered twenty million combat deaths. They are part of this great generation too.

My father was in the Battle of the Coral Sea where the Japanese sunk his ship the aircraft carrier Lexington. The Japanese had designs on the Island of New Guinea from which they could bomb Australia.

The importance of the date September 1st, 1939, when Hitler invaded Poland, is because it caused Great Britain and France to declare war on Germany and begin another war in Europe. Japan had already been waging a genocidal war against the people of China. They dropped the bubonic plague virus from bi-planes over the city of Harbin (the capital of Manchuria) killing countless civilians in 1935. Japan annexed Manchuria and in 1937 they savagely attacked Nanking, now known as Nanjing, in what is known to history as "the rape of Nanking" killing at the very least 200,000 civilians including women and children. Throughout World War II the Japanese experimented on innocent people infecting them with diseases simply to study their bodies' reaction to the torment. It was this appalling behavior on the part of Imperial Japan that prompted the United States to place economic boycotts against the nation of Japan. Japan retaliated with an attack on Pearl Harbor, December 7th 1941.

Since Japan was allied with Germany and Italy, the United States was soon at war with all the Axis powers. The Great War was fought from 1914-1918, with the United States entering the war in 1917. It would now be known to history as World War I. World War II, the sequel, started in China, in 1935.

America wasn't totally unaware that danger was on the horizon. Our aircraft carriers were out to sea scouting for suspicious activity in the waters far south of Pearl Harbor. My father served on the aircraft carrier Lexington. Not he, nor anyone at that time, suspected an attack to come from the north. The Japanese plan of attack was clever, that day. But, later, in May 1942, the American Navy squared off against Imperial Japan in the Coral Sea. The battle was the first action in which aircraft carriers engaged each other, as well as the first in which neither side's ships sighted or fired directly upon the other. Each navy lost some ships and many sailors died. My father's ship, the aircraft carrier Lexington, was severely damaged and scuttled.

Our troops fought bravely, and years later, my father would occasionally talk about it, hustling about in another American way, riding a golf cart. I loved my father. He was a good American. He played golf, even had his own electric golf cart. He said it wasn't because he was lazy but so that he could play more holes before it got dark. He read the box score in the sports section of the newspaper every day until the day heaven took him. He was 81 when he passed.

Dad fought hard in the war, and he cheered mightily for the Saint Louis Cardinals. He favored the National League over the American. He used to take me to Saint Louis to see his beloved Cardinals.

In 1968, I went with my family to Saint Louis. We lived in western Tennessee. Folks there drink Budweiser and they follow the Cardinals. We attended a scheduled double header. My father liked to get his money's worth. We were to see a pitching duel between Jerry Koosman and Bob Gibson. Bob Gibson is now in the hall of fame. But the two didn't pitch against each other. Instead Koosman pitched the first game and Gibson pitched the second. Each game was a one to nothing shut outs. I would have preferred more hitting.

Bobby Tolan hit an inside the park home run in the 1st inning and Bob Gibson made it stand up for the victory in the second game of the day. It was 104 degrees that day with 94% humidity. Four spectators got heat stroke and had to be carried out on stretchers. In those days Missouri allowed 19 year olds to drink. I was 17 but, I have been six feet tall ever since I was in the 8th grade. I guess I looked 19 because I have enjoyed drinking Budweiser ever since.

As the leaves began to fall somewhere in Western Europe ladies in waiting waved silk scarves. They batted their eyes and blushed at a particular knight dressed in shining armor. He is warming up by twirling his sword above his head. He had to be helped up on his horse because of the weight of the armor he wore.

In this jousting contest previously described we have a gray knight helped up on his horse by his squire. His opponent is the beige knight. They each seek the hand of a fair maiden. They each are well practiced in war. They each have defended the land of their fathers from invaders. This contest is mere sport. But they mount their steeds as if going to battle because history has not moved forward to abstract inventions like baseball bats, soccer balls, and bright orange bouncing balls aimed at peach baskets hanging from the rafters. The grey knight spurs his horse and the beige does the same. They raise their spears in an attempt to de-horse the other. It is hoped that only pride will be wounded today. But the games must go on. Men must have sport.

King Henry

Henry II the King of France was struck dead with a lance to the eye during a jousting tournament in 1549. The sport was organized as part of the festivities to celebrate the Peace of Cateau-Cambresis fought mostly in Italy with the Habsburgs of Austria being joined by a

Spanish army. Henry's father Henry I was captured by a Spanish Army fighting in the Piedmont of Italy. He was held prisoner in Spain.

His teen age son, Henry II, was exchanged for his father's release. When young King Henry was returned to France to rule as sovereign he was married in an arrangement made by the families. Henry, however, loved a thirty-five year old woman who had once openly embraced him prior to his captivity in Spain. He married Catherine de' Medici when they were both fourteen years old in 1519. Henry was infatuated with this older woman a thirty-five-year old widow, Diane de Poitiers. Ignoring his wife he would carry the widow's scarf in his jousting competitions. This no doubt infuriated Catherine, but what could she do? Henry was the king. Henry always wore this woman's ribbon and rode as her champion even on his last day in the saddle celebrating the end of the long wars with Austria and Spain.

Jousting continued. Men must have sport. To wish to quell it is as vain a hope as a utopian vision of world without war; or a country where all wealth is shared equally. It is a pipe dream. Mankind loves war much to our chagrin as a species. This is why I champion in this book the notion that sport is war.

Sport, unlike the horror of war, is healthy. It excites us and involves us all either as participant or spectator. For the spectator countless hours can fly by analyzing strategy, while the participants experience the exhilaration of the game itself. Be it football, baseball, basketball, or any other. The participants excel as ath-letes. Societies that lack little league baseball and or A.Y.S.O. soccer are societies where young men make war against each other at an alarming rate. Look to the Middle East and notice the young men armed with mili-tary rifles playing army with deadly consequences.

(2)

Capture the Flag

FOOTBALL PLAYERS LINE up in battle formation wearing their gladiator helmets. They are defending their territory from an invader. The winning team is the team that most often leaves its own territory and invades the other team's terrain. To go to the other team's end zone is to be victorious. Commentators often say "after the reception he took it all the way to the house." The teams employ a shot gun formation. The quarterback is the general on the field. He hopes to bomb the end zone for another score in enemy territory.

When playing golf I might say to my companions, "how shall we attack this green?" Centuries ago a nobleman in Scotland might have employed a squire to carry his golf clubs. Now in prestigious country clubs members can employ a catty. When I attack the green, my aim is to come in high avoiding the bunkers that guard the green. Some greens are completely surrounded by water as a castle would be surrounded by a mote. I carry an array of weapons in my golf bag. Each club is fashioned with a different angle to facilitate my aerial assault. The flag is of course the ultimate goal.

When boys play contact sports sometimes they get carried away and actually start to fight. We never grow up completely. The competitive urges lead us to bench clearing brawls over real and perceived insults. Usually, after pushing and shoving all is quieted down. But other times fists fly. Seen a Hockey game lately?

A professional basketball player named Ron Artest became infamous when he got into a fight with a spectator during a game in Detroit. He has since changed his name to Metta World Peace. We have come a long way from the peach basket hanging from the rafters. Basketball is very popular all over the world.

In the year 1861, (which would see the United States of America divided and engaged in civil war), a Canadian named Dr. James Naismith was born. In 1891 he was an ordained Presbyterian minister teaching physical education at the International YMCA training school in Springfield Massachusetts. He invented basketball deriving the idea from a game called duck on a rock. Originally they used a soccer ball and someone would have to use a ladder to climb up and retrieve the ball after someone made a basket. In 1936 basketball was introduced at the Berlin Olympics. Dr. Naismith presented the medals. The United States got the gold, Canada received silver, and Mexico was awarded the bronze medal.

In America amateur baseball teams competed before the War Between the States. The Cincinnati Red Stockings played in the years directly following the Civil War, and was the first organization to employ professional baseball players. They formed in the winter of 1869, playing their first game in 1870. Other teams competing in that era were the Brooklyn Atlantics, Philadelphia Athletics, and Chicago White Stockings to name a few. My favorite old time name is the Pale Hose also of Chicago. Eventually, the National League was formed in 1875/1876. To this day the National League is called the senior circuit. The American League is often called the Junior Circuit because its inception was twenty five years later in 1901. It may seem arrogant to call the series between National and American League pennant winners the World Series, but seldom do teams from outside the United States win a series of games with American teams.

In Mexico City there is a soccer team called Team America. Mexico is part of the Americas too. The point is still the same. People love sport and sport is preferable to war. Americans invented baseball the way we know it today. Americans invented American Football not soccer. Soccer is a fine game and it too is a substitute for war. All sporting events are.

In September of 2001, America was suffering. We were reeling emotionally from a dastardly attack reminiscent of Pearl Harbor. New Yorkers were feeling it even more than the rest of the country. The attack was local to them. A baseball game proved cathartic when Mike Piazza homered in the bottom of the 8th inning to break a 2-2 tie, and sent the New York crowd home feeling fulfilled having seen their favorite player clobber a ball over the center field wall. It provided the decisive score that would carry the crowd out to the sub-ways and home. The recent events had been horrific. But tonight they had prevailed over the Atlanta Braves. Sherman had burned Atlanta and the Union was preserved figuratively speaking of course. Atlanta ball players, patriots one and all too, remarked later that it was only fitting that the game would end that way. New Yorkers had been through so much. We all have. But right here is where it happened and "right here is where their matinee idol saved the day for their team," Braves third baseman Chipper Jones said in a postgame interview.

From the beginning of time men have fought wars and women have sought security. Yes women seek power too. I am speaking in generalities. Not every man follows baseball or football. But men have always had sport. Native Americans played a game with a stick and a ball. Men rode on horseback racing around a track to see who was fastest. It is called the sport of kings. Some historians give the year 776 B.C. for the first Olympics. Named after Mount Olympus, where the gods lived, the first event was a foot race only 600 feet long. I guess we would call it a sprint. Discus, javelin, long jump, and wrestling were soon added. Later a few different length foot races were added.

Saint Paul mentions running the race for a laurel wreath in his letter to the Corinthians. Paul writes: *Do you not know that in a race all the runners run, but only one gets the prize? Run in such a way as to get the prize...* They do it to get a crown that will not last; but we do it to get a crown that will last forever. Therefore I do not run like a man running aimlessly. (1 Corinthians 9:24-26 NIV). Run to win. Don't run aimlessly but with your eyes on the prize.

In 1956, the Hungarian people wanted to be free of the repression the Soviet Union imposed upon them. A revolution ensued. James Michener was living in Austria in the 1950's. The Bridge at Andau chronicles the struggle for freedom the brave men and women pursued against a hated occupier. The bridge is a border crossing place leading to Austria and freedom.

In my life I have known a few men that came out of Hungary at this time in history. A machinist I worked with in Phoenix, Arizona once told me that when he was a boy at the end of World War II Russian soldiers occupied his home. They had never seen indoor plumbing. The men had caught a pretty big trout in the river and were looking for a place to clean the fish. They placed it in the toilet to scale it. One of them said "What does this handle do?" He pulled the handle, my friend told me, "and woosh no more fish." He told me he laughed at them and they got mad. This is a reminder of how fortunate we are to live in America and have a constitution that protects us from having soldiers living in our homes.

Most people in this world have no such protections. In modern times, it seems to me too many people have lost sight of how fortunate we Americans are. Freedom is not free.

In 1956 in Budapest, Hungry ordinary people fought Soviet tanks with wine bottles filled with gasoline and a match. The "Molotov cocktail" was so named originally by the Fins to mock Soviet Foreign Minister Vyacheslav Molotov during the Winter War in Finland in 1939. Molotov and the Nazi German Foreign Minister Joachim von Ribbentrop signed an agreement known to history as the Non-Aggression Pact between Germany and the Soviet Union. This pact precipitated the partition of Poland and the invasion of Finland among other things.

In 1956 in Buda-Pest, Hungarian women were seen using a mops to spread soap over cobble stone streets. This caused the tanks to lose traction and crash into the walls of ancient buildings where men and woman could poor gasoline on them and set them on fire. People were seen putting Hungarian flags on Russian tanks hoping the enemy would destroy their own tank. In the end forty thousand were dead and the iron curtain remained closed until the Berlin wall came down in 1989. Now Hungary is in NATO. I would never have believed it in the sixties, when, I read Bridge at Andau back in high school.

My friends and I were visiting the Grand Canyon. Their names were Ned and Janet. They were from Australia. This was during the same time I knew the man from Hungary. But these people were from down under not Austria. We were staying in a modest lodge in the National Park. If you have never been there you are missing something special. So we were going hiking. But first, why not go to the El Tovar Hotel to get a better look at the canyon from inside the bar and restaurant? The United States of America was playing Olympic Hockey against the Soviet Union. Since the game was tied, we decided to order more beers and watch it for a while.

What we witnessed might be the greatest single sporting event of all time. Younger readers may be excused if you do not realize how things used to be during the Cold War. In America and throughout the world the Olympic commission insisted on amateur athletes. Professionals were banned. This meant no dream team in basketball and likewise no National Hockey League players. We sent our college teams.

America would select an all-star team of college athletes to go to the Olympics and compete. In Hockey, Basketball, Water Polo, team Tennis, you name it. The communist country's, like Russia, kept the same players together through several Olympic seasons playing together as a team. They practiced together. They traveled the world together playing in various competitions for over a decade. They got very good because of this. They were not considered profession-als because in the Soviet Union they did not receive any money for playing their sport. No one received any money because the State controlled everything. They (the State) paid their housing, and they provided their meals. They paid for their transportation throughout the first, second, and third worlds. So they really were professional. This was all they did. They did not have other jobs.

The State selected the more gifted athletes, male and female, and steered them into sports to represent the Nation for the greater glory of the cause of communism. This put the United States, and other teams, at a tremen-dous disadvantage. Yet, somehow, in 1980, our amateurs beat them fair and square on the ice in Lake Placid, New York. My friends and I saw the whole thing live from the El Tovar Hotel, at the rim of the Grand Canyon.

Mankind is constantly competing. We compete for resources. We compete for admiration and even love. All of us are competitive. Ancient Greeks stopped their warring long enough to hold the Olympic Games. Our focus here is on our (mankind's) history as a species of war and aggression. We celebrate how these impulses are transformed into the exhilarating joy of organized competitive sports.

The American Civil War has been called by some the noblest war ever undertaken. In antebellum America and post war America Americans were blessed with more leisure time than any society had ever known here-to-fore. Our ancestors here in the states could rise in the morning and read the newspaper describing the Lincoln / Douglas debates. And they would begin to read about the national pass time. The highlights of the home team's victory or loss were chronicled, each and every day, just as it is to this day.

We have the "box score" - the statistical record of the player's performance in a given game. This competition was organized into professional baseball, in 1870, when the city of Cincinnati decided to pay their players in order to defend the honor of the city. Once this started, it took more than a year for the Cincinnati baseball team to be defeated. Soon the National League was formed to organize this competition. At the turn of the twentieth century there were so many professional baseball teams that the American League was created. It would be said that the leader of each league, at the conclusion of the season, had won the pennant, and should play the other league's champion in the World Series to determine the champion.

As children, we play capture the flag. As adults, we play golf or tennis. We spend countless hours and countless dollars learning to analyze baseball strategies and fantasy football strategies. American football is so war like in its approach that the metaphor of war is plain to see. In hockey one must defend his goal.

In baseball, we move from base to base where we are safe. But it counts for nothing unless we make it to home plate. A soldier could survive the battle of

Shiloh, Vicksburg, and New Orleans but not make it home safely. When we are home safe we score a run, a point, a tally.

The hot summer of 1861 wore on. The Union army had only to go a hundred miles south, capture Richmond, and bring this terrible civil war to an end. But their countrymen to the south had other ideas. They saw themselves as part of a different country. They saw their leader Robert E. Lee as another George Washington fighting for their rights, and defending their homes and property, and their women from alien invaders. We spoke the same language. We believed in the same God. Often each side lined up in rows the way they were taught that the foolish red coats did four score and seven years before. The pride and gallantry these men possessed inspires writers of history to this day.

War can be tedious. The countless hours of marching, and waiting and waiting, can be dreary. On both sides of the Mason Dixon line men would step off 90-feet between bases, and place something like a sack of flour in a diamond shape. Someone would find a bat and ball and a game would begin. "Three strikes and you're out." "That's four wide ones soldier. Take your base. " The crack of the bat is much preferred to the crack of a rifle. Analyzing the hit and run is greatly favored morally to the planning of an ambush that could start a revolution.

(3)

Shiloh

WHEN I WAS a boy I lived in Mississippi. Once I took an overnight trip with the boy scouts to Shiloh National Battle Field. My fascination with the American Civil War probably began then. We rode in a school bus across the state line to the place in Tennessee the Union had called Pittsburg Landing. It is better known to history as Shiloh. Most battle fields during the War Between the States had a Southern and a Northern name. The Confederates named a battle after the nearest town. While the Union would name a battlefield after the nearest body of water; this is why there is Manassas and Bull Run. Antietam and Sharpsburg is another example.

At Pittsburg Landing, on the Tennessee River, only a few miles north of the Tennessee border with Mississippi, there is a church, Shiloh Church. Grant ordered Sherman to make camp and await the arrival of Buell's Army of the Ohio coming from Nashville. It is a poor military tactic to have your back against a river. There is no retreat if things turn sour. Grant and Sherman were overconfident.

The Confederates controlled a major railroad junction in Corinth, Mississippi. This railroad junction was the Union Army Commander's objective. Future American President Ulysses S. Grant commanded the Army of the Tennessee. He intended to control the Tennessee River by the end of the war. Grant had already used this river to great effect and would continue to do so.

Albert Sidney Johnston commanded the Confederate Army of Mississippi, which was named, not for the river the way the Union armies were designated, but rather the state or the region. Johnston conceived a plan of attack, launched from Corinth. It was to seize Pittsburg Landing and destroy the Union Army camped there

We boy scouts went on a long, exhausting hike covering many miles. Then, we were led to a museum where many interesting artifacts still exist. The University of Tennessee has produced an informative documentary demonstrating the tactics employed by the opposing armies. They use maps and actors to teach the history of the event. The valor, the courage, the determination, and the deadly seriousness of the conflict was driven home to this eleven year old visiting that day.

General Johnston, on the Confederate side, believed that the South could not match the manpower of the Union army. His thinking was that by consolidating southern troops deeper in the south, away from the Yankee supply lines, a Confederate victory might be achieved. Even though the Confederates were out-numbered, the relative sizes of the armies were similar. The Union camped with their backs to the Tennessee River, awaiting a second army marching overland from Nashville. This army, commanded by General Buell, was called the Army of the Ohio, after the river from which they came. The Confederates hoped to destroy the Union army before they could be joined. It almost worked. Grant and his soldiers were caught completely by surprise. But the union army in this place was not made up of city slickers. They were pioneer types from Iowa and Illinois. They fought tenaciously in a place called the sunken road behind a picket fence.

Wave after wave of southerners were repulsed with rifle fire. Later, the soldiers called this place "the hornet nest". Albert Sidney Johnston directing his men ordered his personal surgeon to "go where brave men were fighting and dying". When his doctor returned, he found his commander slumped on his horse. He had been struck in the leg with a riffle ball. He bled to death soon after.

The generals of this age never fully recognized the deadliness of riffle fire as compared to musket fire. This was especially true in the first year of our American tragedy. The accuracy, and in this case, the greater range of what even trained soldiers were used to, far exceeded their imagination in 1862.

The defenders of the sunken road were finally forced to retreat after the Confederates consolidated their cannons and drove the remaining defenders to the river's edge. Thousands sat cowering on the banks of the Tennessee River at the landing as darkness fell. When darkness came the fighting stopped. The Confederacy lost their opportunity to gain a major victory in the western theatre of operations. It was April. Had it been June or July the daylight would probably have lasted long enough for a complete and humiliating defeat of Generals' Sherman and Grant. This would have prolonged the war quite a bit. It would not have won the war of succession for the Confederacy. The Union would have had to find other generals to do what was necessary to reunite the country. Grant and Sherman would have been disgraced.

But someone else would have risen to prominence and led the nation's armies to victory over the rebellious southern men at arms. Grant having survived his mistake

at Shiloh would prove himself to be a brilliant general in Mississippi. Grant had 77,000 troops in Mississippi compared to the Confederate's 33,000 defending Vicksburg. In a bold move, he captured the State's capital, Jackson, and then he decided to lay siege to Vicksburg. Vicksburg surrendered on July 4th 1863. It was the day after the battle of Gettysburg had concluded far away in Pennsylvania.

Union casualties were relatively light (4,800) at Vicksburg. The Confederates were forced to surrender an entire army of approximately 29,000 soldiers, officers and men. They were starving.

Sherman would go on to capture Atlanta, Georgia, and oversee his famous march to the sea on the Atlantic coast. He then swung north and marched his army through South Carolina, where the rebellion had begun, and went on to North Carolina too by the war's end.

Out on the battlefield, at Shiloh church, men were moaning in pain. Many would bleed to death before help arrived. Some would live to fight another day.

Fortunately, for the Union, reinforcements arrived that very night. The gunboats accompanying the Army of the Tennessee kept up a constant barrage all through the night. Few were injured by the shelling but, the southern soldiers were denied the rest and sleep they so desperately needed.

The reinforcements that arrived by gunboat that night had to push their way ashore through the throngs of men who refused to move. The men on the dock and on the shore were paralyzed with fear after what they had seen on the battlefield that day. These men warned the fresh soldiers that certain death awaited them if they did not turn back. Officers threatened to shoot soldiers that were blocking the way of the re-enforcements that were trying to disembark, and the seas of cowering men parted. With fresh troops arriving, in the form of the Army of Ohio, ferried across the Tennessee River by the before mentioned gunboats, the Confederate army had no hope of winning this battle. They were so outnumbered. By many accounts, after the re-enforcements General Buell brought with him the Confederate army was outnumbered by twenty thousand. Each side had lost 1,700 killed and over 20,000 total casualties had been inflicted, Americans all north and south.

American football, both college and professional is extremely popular in our country. Nowhere is football more popular than in the south. I believe football is so very popular in the south because both teams have an equal number of contestants (11) when they meet on the grid iron.

When Michigan State comes to play Mississippi State there are only eleven men allowed on the field for each side. During the holidays there are a few college all-star games East vs.: West and North vs.: South but the game that stimulates my imagination is the Blue Gray game.

When Robert E. Lee took the Army of Northern Virginia to Gettysburg, Pennsylvania he had 71,000 men. George G. Meade, commanding the Army of the Potomac, had 91,000. And Meade was on the defensive. Each side suffered 23,000 causalities or 46,000 combined. Were there good guys and bad guys in this war? Could this war have been avoided? I do not know if it could have been avoided. I only know that it *should* have been avoided.

But at what cost could history wait? How long could a nation conceived in liberty based on the premise that all men are created equal allow the buying and selling of other men?

Still it is important to remember that most southerners only saw that an army was coming to destroy their land. Their farms would be burned and their livestock taken. Their loved ones could be raped or killed. In the world of 1861, few nations on the face of the globe had outlawed slavery. France and England had banned slavery a generation earlier than the United States. But few other countries on earth had followed suit outside of Western Europe.

Most of the country saw the War Between the States as a duty to preserve the Union. America is the best hope of the entire world. If we had been torn in two in the 1860's, we might not have been strong enough to stop the Nazi's and Imperial Japan from their genocidal conquests.

(4)

American Excellence

FOOTBALL

IN THE LATER part of the 19th century, a man named Walter Camp made a drastic change to the game of rugby. Rugby was an English game played in America. Camp, born in Connecticut and a graduate of Yale, introduced "the line of scrimmage". Football began to be popular at American institutions of higher education. In 1892, William "Pudge" Heffelfinger was paid $500 to play football for the Allegheny Athletic Association against the Pittsburgh Athletic Club. In the 1920's, legendary coaches such as Knute Rockne and Pop Warner advanced the popularity of a new wrinkle, the forward pass.

I enjoy both college and pro football. I am a USC Trojan fan and a San Diego Charger fan. The analogies with land acquisition through war are obvious. You defend your goal and you attack your opponent's land. When you line up your soldiers, you probe for a weakness. In football, pushing two blockers forward can punch a hole in the defense -- allowing the ball carrier to split the seam now created, and get into the backfield flanking your opponent, and making his defenders useless. As you march relentlessly to the castle protected only by a borderline of chalk spread across the grass; he is yours. You have won. American Football is the ultimate war game.

BASEBALL

In antebellum America baseball was already popular. I have seen a political cartoon showing Abraham Lincoln holding a baseball bat. During the Civil War soldiers played baseball games. 1st platoon might play 2nd platoon and so forth. Before the war, most folks didn't go far from their homes their whole lives. But the war changed that. After Grant took the Army of Tennessee down the Mississippi river to Vicksburg, and Sherman, who was also at Shiloh, marched from Chattanooga to Atlanta and on to the sea; many American soldiers had seen quite a bit of our rather large and beautiful country. The knowledge of the game spread.

BABE RUTH

They called it the curse of the Bambino. In 1918, the Boston Red Sox had a pitcher, yes a pitcher, named

Babe Ruth. The Red Sox won the World Series that season. Inexplicably the team sold the contract of Ruth to their big city rival, the New York Yankees. The Yankees were an original American League Franchise. They started out in 1901, in Baltimore, as the Baltimore Orioles. They moved to New York City in 1903, and changed their name to the Highlanders. In 1913, they adopted the name Yankees. The Yankees offered cash money to the Red Sox for the right to own the baseball contract of George Herman Ruth. They didn't trade him for another player. They just sold him like Joseph's brothers sold Joseph into slavery to an Egyptian caravan passing by.

Even though Herman was an excellent pitcher, the Yankees took note of what a good hitter he was. They decided his bat was too potent to miss so many games. Pitchers put so much stress on their arms pitching at the major league level that they require time off to recuperate after pitching a game. In modern times, they traditionally get four days off between starts. In 1918, Babe hit 11 home runs as a pitcher for the Red Sox. In 1919, he hit 29, an astronomical amount for the era. In 1920, his first year with the Yankees, Ruth hit 54 homeruns. So the legend of the "babe" was born. He hit 60 home runs in 1927. They call Yankee stadium the house that Ruth built because he put so many butts in the seats.

In 2012, the Oakland Athletics had won the American League Western Division and stood ready to seize the pennant. (They have one of the smallest payrolls in baseball.) This caused much excitement in baseball circles. They had to go through the New York Yankees who have the highest payroll in baseball. But games are played on a baseball diamond. No matter how much or how little you are paid; you still have to hit the ball. And someone else has to catch it.

In the war rooms around major league baseball, new managers are being discussed. Poor Bobby Valentine was dismissed the first day after the season ended. Terry Francona led the Boston Red Sox to two World Series victories, the first championship since 1918. This finally broke the curse of the Bambino. The Red Sox went to the World Series a handful of times in the interim period only to be defeated by their National League opponent. People believed the curse of the Bambino was alive and well. But Francona and his troops overcame all the obstacles. They overcame the psychological obstacles, physical obstacles, and the New York Yankees.

A couple years later they were back defeating the National League rival 4 games to none. But then with the second highest payroll, second only to the New York Yankees, they failed to make the play-offs. They missed the cut by one game and ownership in Boston called for a change at the helm. They fired Terry Francona and replaced him with Bobby Valentine. Valentine has an excellent baseball mind. But apparently he was not a good fit in Boston. Eliminated from the play-offs, the Red Sox had one of the worst seasons in franchise history.

With a one day lull before the battle which would begin October 5th, 2012 between rival American League teams involved in the post season, the Red Sox fired Bobby Valentine. Sport is war. The war between Boston and New York flows over to every team sport. The Patriots and the Jets have a big rivalry. The Knickerbockers and the Celtic have a heated rivalry. Get on your horse Paul Revere. Bostonians must find a new general.

(5)

Gangues Khan

LEARNED AN IMMEASURABLE amount of world history from the James Michener books I have consumed. Poland is about European history. In Poland, Michener recounts how when Gangues Khan conquered the Ukraine, he ordered everyone taller than a wagon wheel slain. He might have said. "We will raise the children as our own with our own customs and our own religion."

Consider this: men love sport, and in fact simply must pursue it. What about women: loving nice clothes and expensive jewelry? Imagine the feeling of dread when the Tartars came. A brief battle would occur with a few villagers fighting for their lives trying in vain to protect their

belongings and their loved ones. When the defenders with weapons were all slain, a commanding officer would order the roundup all the villagers to put them to the sword. But before carrying out the Khan's directive he might have said "not this one; she is very beautiful." And then his eyes fall upon another unfortunate woman far less fair. Indeed plain beyond noticing except the commander says to his lieutenant "and spare her too."

"Your Excellency you would spare her too?"

"Yes, I fancy the necklace around her neck. Bring her to my tent as well."

This explains why women collect jewelry and men collect baseball cards. It is primordial in our nature. From the beginning of time men have fought wars and women have sought security. I am speaking in generalities. Yes, women seek power too. And not everyman follows baseball or football. But men have always had sport.

Native Americans played a game with a stick and a ball. Men rode on horseback racing around a track to see who was fastest. It is called the sport of kings. Women collect evening gowns and men collect fishing lures.

The year 2012, there was a soccer competition called the European Cup. The host countries were Poland and the Ukraine. My dear friend is from Kiev. She is an American now; her name is Oksana like the gold metal

Olympic Ice Skater. She sent me a text to let me know that Ukraine had a game coming up against Sweden, to be played where she was born in Kiev. I started following the competition. Ukraine defeated Sweden, but then, later, fell to France.

I saw on the news that there was some trouble in Poland. Protesters raised angry fists when the Russian team arrived. Many still hold a grudge about the long years behind the iron curtain. Others on the other side of this political divide, long for the return of communism, and a return to the way things were for seventy years. Soccer riots are far too common in the world. But during these games, the only violence I saw on the news was at this demonstration and counter demonstration in Poland. These demonstrations occurred before one of the games.

The worst example of fan violence, I know of, is the story of the poor fellow that was shot to death in Columbia because he accidently kicked the ball in his own goal.

THIS ISN'T A FOOTBALL GAME

When I was a teen-ager I read Fail Safe twice. Fail Safe, the book and the movie, starring Henry Fonda, was no comedy. I was struck by the potential for real life tragedy. As the story unfolded, a squadron of American jet bombers carrying a nuclear payload flew to their predetermined co-ordinance. It was at this place where they should have been recalled, having found that this was just another false alarm caused by a flock of Canadian geese or sun spots or something that caused our radar system to sound the alarm, sending our planes soaring into the heavens. But something went wrong, and they lost radio contact.

By the time they could re-establish radio contact, from the United States to the aircraft, it was too late. They had been trained not to turn back under any circumstances. It might be a trick they were told. When the Pentagon got the pilot's wife on the radio, in the movie she was hysterical; the pilot says to his crew, "I wonder how they got someone to imitate my wife's voice." The pilot and his entire squadron were determined to fly on to Moscow and drop their deadly munitions. The Americans then alerted the Russian as to what was happening.

The Russians were skeptical, of course, but little-by-little they began to believe the American President as he explained that it was all a horrible mistake. He spoke to them on the famous "hot line" the red telephone linking Washington and Moscow.

The American's begin giving away their secrets in radar avoidance in order to aid the Russians in shooting down the American bombers. Considering the unspeakably serious nature of this scenario, it's no wonder that, upon seeing how the men in the war room in

Omaha began to cheer as one-by-one the blips begin to disappear from the radar screen, the general steps into the room, barking "Stop that at once! This isn't a football game!"

(6)

Analysis

SPORT IS A good substitute for actual war. We love sporting events. We plan and we plot. We analyze and we strategize. We cheer and we applaud. We relish the competition. Whether it is a chess match, a tennis match, the World Cup, or the Super Bowl we love it with the intensity of battle. But war is not sport. Throughout the ages kings and others have moved their soldiers about as if in a game simply for their vanity. These leaders have held little regard for the life and limb of the soldiers ordered about like pawns on a chess board by their sovereigns. I have focused on the few wars where a colossal moral imperative was at stake.

Ambrose Burnside was at Antietam Creek the day General George McClellan let Robert E. Lee's army escape defeat. McClellan's indecisiveness and timidity resulted in the tragedy that is the American Civil War going on from the day of the battle in 1862 until April 1865. Another three years of carnage might have been cut in half by a decisive victory in Sharpsburg, Maryland, that day. Later, Lincoln would use that place to give a speech and issue the emancipation proclamation. Ambrose Burnside was there witnessing this indecisiveness. He realized that if the Union Army had committed all their strength that day the war in the East might have been decided. The North so vastly outnumbered the South on the battle field that day that any trained officer should have been able to grasp the opportunity. The Union men at arms totaled 75,000 where-as the Confederate Army had 38,000. Burnside, a field commander that day, sent wave after wave of men to near certain death across a narrow bridge that now bears his name. After many attempts, the army of the Potomac seized the ground across the bridge. The other Union battalions were coming on the rebels from the north. It was then that fresh Confederate reinforcement arrived in quantities capable of stemming the tide of the Northern advance, giving Robert E. Lee and his Army of Northern Virginia a chance to retreat across the Potomac and back to Virginia.

McClellan claimed a great victory. It was here President Lincoln announced his famous emancipation proclamation: freeing all the slaves in the territories of the rebellion. He did not free the slaves at this time in the non-rebelling states, the so called Border States, such as Maryland where he was standing. It would take the 13th Amendment to free all Americans.

Later, Lincoln fired McClellan. He promoted Ambrose Burnside and his sideburns to commander and chief of the Army of the Potomac. Burnside was determined to smash Robert E. Lee's army with his superior numbers. He lamented the missed opportunity when the rebels advanced north into Maryland and away from their supplies. True, the rebels had taken a defensive position occupying the town of Sharpsburg, using Antietam Creek as a defensive barrier to hinder the Northern advance, but this was not much protection from the numerous Northern guns and troops.

At the battle of Fredericksburg the rebels were well situated behind the broad Rappahannock River, on a steep hillside where stood the Virginia town of Fredericksburg. The North had 120,000 men at arms where-as the south had 80,000. But the defensive position was impregnable. To make things worse, the boats the north intended to use had been delayed by several days defeating any element of surprise. The Union army should have moved the entire army to one flank or the other, completely ignoring that position. It would have forced the confederates off of the hill and onto more suitable ground for a Union advance. But Burnside was determined to use his numerical superiority to overwhelm the Confederates the way he realized McClellan should have at Sharpsburg.

Abner Doubleday was on the field of battle that day. It is a good thing that he wasn't killed as so many were because history has given him credit for the invention of baseball. On this day, Doubleday was part of the Union's army of the Potomac. He prepared to cross the Rappahannock, and to charge up the hill right into the Confederate guns.

As the Northern men were being cut down like wheat with a scythe, Robert E. Lee was heard to have said to James Longstreet "it is good that war is so terrible lest we come to love it too much." Well, I am afraid to report that it was too late for Robert E. Lee. I believe he had already come to love it too much. His idealism and devotion to the southern cause led him to kill in war more Americans then Rommel and Hideki Tojo in the Second World War. Indeed, all are wars combined do not equal the casualties of the War Between the States.

THE SHOT HEARD AROUND THE WORLD

The musket volley at the start of the American revolutionary war is known to history as the "shot heard around the world." Those musket blasts were the death knell for the concept of the divine right of kings. The line is originally from the opening stanza of Ralph Waldo Emerson's "Concord Hymn" (1837), and referred to the beginning of the American Revolutionary War.

This 1775 first shot was fired during an armed stand-off between British forces and local militia in Lexington, escalating into engagements at the Old North Bridge in the battles of Lexington and Concord. It started a chain of events which subsequently led to the signing of the Declaration of Independence and the Thirteen Colonies achieving independence from Britain. Men have inalienable rights and Kings put on their trousers one leg at a time just like every other man does.

"The Giants win the pennant, the giants win the pennant, the giants win the pennant, the giants win the pennant; Bobbie Thompson hits into the lower deck, the giants win the pennant and they are going crazy, they're going crazy they are..."

The Giants win the pennant is one of the most famous radio and television broadcast in sports history. The Brooklyn Dodgers had a huge lead over the New York Giants with about a month to play. But the Giants kept getting closer, and by the last day of the season they were tied. Booby Thompson hit a ninth inning home run to vanquish the Dodgers and win the pennant for the Giants. In baseball parlances, Bobby Thompson's home run is referred to as the "shot heard around the world." That was in 1951 the very year I was born.

There is an episode on MASH that spotlights this event. I don't know about you, but I feel differently about the so called "police action" in Korea then I do about the "police action" in Vietnam. The United Nations voted on a resolution to send peace keepers to the Korean peninsula. In Vietnam there was a treaty called S.E.A.T.O. (South East Asia Treaty Organization). This treaty was flawed to my way of thinking, but it still was a treaty that had to be honored until other arrangements could be negotiated.

Korea was more clear cut. With the United Nations involvement, the United States took up the cause of the white knight. North Korea had invaded seeking to unify the country under communist totalitarianism. The south resisted militarily. General Douglas MacArthur devised one of the most impressive and creative military maneuvers in history. MacArthur's soldiers and marines made a successful landing at Inchon, deep behind North Korean lines. Launched with naval and close air support, the landing outflanked the North Koreans, recaptured Seoul and forced them to retreat northward in disarray. It was a classic end around football coaches could admire. With a little bit of miss-direction for diversion MacArthur's men landed at Inchon and saved South Korea from being occupied by a communist dictator.

THE BEIGE KNIGHT

In Vietnam, America was playing the role of the beige knight. Our intentions were good. We, as always in our history, wanted to help an oppressed people. But help at what cost? What was the cost to America, and how about the terrible cost to the suffering people we were trying to help?

So many people died in Indo-China as a result of constant war from World War II until 1975. Thirty years passed with no solution, only more and more suffering. If you fought there, hold your head up. You did your duty for your country. You did what the leaders of this usually noble country asked you to do.

As for myself I believe in God. I attend church regularly on Sunday. The Bible says "thou shalt not kill." I interpret that to mean thou shalt not murder. If you take up arms, and follow your call to duty as a patriot in a war there will be killing, but this is not murder.

However my conscience led me to a different belief about the Vietnam conflict for myself. I believed that America was never going to win the Vietnam War. Some say America could have won the Vietnam War if we had really tried. Maybe so; but still, the point is America was never going to win that war. We were never going to declare war. In fact America has not declared war since 1941. Without a declaration of all-out war, "winning" the Vietnam "police action" was never going to happen.

How could I raise my rifle to my eye and kill a man in a war I knew my country was not going to win? To kill a man with that sure knowledge would be murder. When General Picket led his men across open ground at Gettysburg he trusted Robert E. Lee's judgment. He later said "that old man destroyed my army." General Longstreet knew Lee was making a mistake, but he still believed the Confederacy would eventually prevail. I knew it was futile to fight on in Vietnam when I registered for the draft in 1970.

I am so proud of my father, and his service in WW II and Korea. I wish I could have been part of something great when I was 19. Those who have served in Afghanistan have helped to make the world a better place. And now we have killed Bin Laden. But Vietnam is the same place now it always was destined to be. Our 58,000 young men died for nothing. And worse yet they killed for nothing. I work with men from Vietnam. They go home every year at Christmas. My old boss Dan is a Quality Assurance Manager and he is an Anglo like me. Dan went there on his vacation.

In Afghanistan, we are building baseball diamonds. Boys and girls are playing little league baseball and they are learning to read. The anarchy that passed for government in Afghanistan attacked us on 9/11. It is the closest thing my generation will ever have to knowing what it must have been like to have been an American the day after Pearl Harbor was bombed. We were all together. The whole world was behind us when we went to Afghanistan. There was so much good will toward America, internationally, at that time.

Then, George Bush threw it all away when he ordered an attack on Iraq and our clueless congress went along with it Democrats and Republicans alike. If our efforts in Afghanistan proved to be fruitless it will be because America took her eye off of the ball and invaded Iraq. It pains me to see America so polarized. Thank God we have sports to bring us together.

WHATEVER LOLA WANTS LOLA GETS.

All of Washington D.C. was proud of the Nationals when they made the play-offs. And they all shared the disappointment when Saint Louis snatched victory away from them in the 9th inning. The Nationals were ahead by 6 runs after 3 innings. Going into the top of the 9th inning, they were still ahead by 2 runs. The Cardinals got 4 runs in their final at bat, and sent a stunned crowd home with some crying from disappointment. After all, it has been a long time for Washington.

The old Washington Senators were an American League Team. They had been in the World Series in 1933. Their only World Championship was in 1924 when hall of fame pitcher Walter Johnson, nick named "the train", lost both of the games he'd started. Game seven went into an extra inning and "the train" pitched 4 scoreless innings to earn the victory over the Giants for the Senators only World Series Championship.

The Broadway musical "Damned Yankees" opened on Broadway in 1955. It is the story of an old man's fanatical obsession with his team the Washington Senators.

They were always losing the pennant to the New York Yankees. He would do anything to see them in the World Series just once. So he sells his soul to the devil in a Faustian bargain that makes him young and strong again. As well as young and strong, he is one of the most gifted baseball players the country has ever seen.

Remember the song "whatever Lola wants Lola gets...?" The devil sends a beautiful young woman to seduce our hero and keep him in line. In the end he tries to save his soul, and the devil turns him back into an old man while he is standing in the outfield at his position. He is unable to catch a fly ball and the Yankees win again. He runs off the field and no one ever sees him again.

The Senators moved to Minnesota and became the Twins. Washington didn't have a team for many years. Then the Montreal Expos of the National League moved their franchise to Washington and changed their name to the Nationals. As this book is being written, and our leaders in Washington are contemplating driving the whole nation over the fiscal cliff, it's the same ole' "we'll get em next year" for baseball fans of Washington D.C.

I was watching the television show called the Hot Stove when Mitch Williams said; "I hate it when players and coaches talk about the game as if it was a war." His point was that to do so is to do a dis-service to the men and women fighting for our freedom around the world. This point is well taken. As I have pointed out war is not sport. But the passion sports fans burn with is transference of competitive and sometimes violent impulses, into a healthy exuberance. This zeal has all the characteristics of jingoistic idealism channeled in a harmless yet exhilarating way.

The time and energy spent by the participant on both armature and professional athletics is enormous. Yet these numbers are dwarfed by the number of people involved in the media's reporting of our various sports' interest. And still, there are the rest of us that read the newspapers, buy the periodicals, and watch the cable television broadcast. People listening to the radio and watching on television to follow their local teams comprise the lion's share of sports fans. These fans vastly outnumber the amount of fans that actually buy a ticket to a live event.

Radio is still a huge source of revenue for a baseball franchise. Major and Minor League baseball games are prevalent on the radio. I listen to a radio broadcast streaming through my lap top while I am writing. I can obtain a televised feed on my lap top as well. But I am satisfied with the radio. Baseball, Football, Basketball, and Hockey are very entertaining on the radio. Just the same, it is my opinion that the enormous amounts of money generated by television contracts is what drives the million dollar contracts reported on today in all the sports. These numbers are obscene. It distresses me to read about contracts of 20 million a year for playing a game. The owners cry poverty in every sport. All I can say is that someone would not offer someone else twenty million dollars if they could not afford it. Why would anyone say no to a multi-million dollar contract? These star athletes are the new Princes of the earth.

(7)

Tennis

SOME HISTORIANS TRACE the origins of tennis before the year 1000 to the Egyptian town of Tinnis, on the river Nile, and the origin of the word "racquet" to the Arabic word for palm – rahat. Stronger historical evidence tracks tennis to the crude handball game of 11th and 12th century France. French monks played a game like handball they called *jeu de paume* or "game of the hand." But the bouncing ball was centuries away. The French monks played with a ball made of wound hair.

In **1874:** Major Walter Wingfield was awarded a British patent for the game of tennis. Two brothers, William and Ernest Renshaw, dominated Wimbledon in the 1880's.

Nearly a century later, the fiery Jimmy Connors and the stoic and lovely Chris Evert, employed a two-fisted backhand and flat-ball baseline game. The other great champion of the era is: Sweden's Bjorn Borg, who established a record in a relatively short career, as one of the all-time greats.

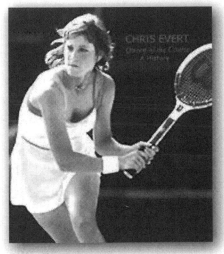

More than that, Borg became the first "rock-star" and mega-bucks tennis player. Later, known for his temper, New Yorker John McEnroe would rise to the top in tennis circles. Arthur Ashe was the first black tennis professional to win Wimbledon in 1975.

On the women's side, Czech Martina Navratilova emerged near the end of the 70s. Tracy Austin won her first U.S. Open in 1979 and a second in 1981. She was only 26 years old when she was involved in a car accident in New Jersey that forced her to give up the game she loved.

Currently, as in the beginning, the siblings are dominating the game. Two sisters: Serena and Venus Williams have established a new standard for the power baseline game in women's tennis. Serena has amassed 12 Grand Slam singles titles, and Venus 7 Grand Slam singles titles.

There is a cultural gentleness about the game of tennis. It is sort of nice that when you announce your score rather than saying I have 2 and you have zero or nothing in tennis you say; "I have 30 and you have love."

Chris Evert is a very charming former tennis champion. Jim Rome, the sports commentator, made himself famous by instigating a fight with Rams quarterback Jim Everett by constantly calling the football player Chris until Jim struck the interviewer. Chris can be seen analyzing tennis on television these days. I seldom watch tennis, but I do enjoy her commentary.

Billy Jean King was a women's champion tennis player back in the day. She won the Australian Open, French Open, Wimbledon, and the U.S. Open. Well, there was this blow hard named Bobby Riggs. He went out of his way to make controversial sexist comments in an attempt to draw attention to himself. And it worked. He and Billy Jean King squared off in a televised and highly publicized tennis match, billed the Battle of the Sexes, in 1973. Billy won the match, and her career moved on. In 1987 she was inducted into the tennis hall of fame. Here again we had a symbolic battle. It was billed as the war between the sexes. It got folks stirred up. Riggs was 55 and King only 29. It was more a contest of youth versus experience, to my mind, than a battle of the sexes, but it is history now. An estimated 90 million watched on T.V., with 30,000 in attendance, live in the Houston Astro Dome. It is the largest audience ever to see a tennis match live still to this day.

(8)

The Great Northwest

NOTRE DAME PLAYED their first college football game in 1897, against the University of Michigan. In 1918, the year the Great War ended in Europe, Knute Rockne, Notre Dame's greatest coach, began his tenure. He would win 105 games, losing only 12, and tying 5, before dying in a plane crash, in 1931. He was only 43. He is perhaps most famous for his speech encouraging his players to "win one for the gipper". Notre Dame had a player named George Gipp. His nick name was "the gipper." George Gipp played football for Notre Dame and was coached by Knute Rockne.

In 1928, Army was undefeated when they met Notre Dame's Fighting Irish. Army is called the Black Knights. Army was leading at the half when Knute gave his now famous speech. He told his team that before George Gipper passed away he said: ***"I've got to go, Rock. It's all right. I'm not afraid. Some time, Rock, when the team is up against it, when things are going wrong*** *and the breaks are beating the boys, tell them to go in there with all they've got and win just one for the Gipper. I don't know where I'll be then, Rock. But I'll know about it, and I'll be happy."*

Notre Dame, a prestigious school is in South Bend, Indiana. Notre Dame is currently coached by Brian Kelly. Brian Kelly helped put a here-to-fore little recognized Cincinnati Bears Cats football team on the college football map, gaining for them: Bowl eligibility and national respect. Brian Kelly caught the attention of the Notre Dame alumni. They offered him a contract in 2010.

This season, the Fighting Irish went undefeated in 2012. In 2013, they played in the Orange Bowl for the right to be called the number one team in college football. They were 12 and 0. They were playing 2nd ranked Alabama Crimson Tide. The Tide has the most national championships and Notre Dame has the second most. It was to be a classic match-up of the north against the south. However the game got out of hand quickly for the fighting Irish."

My family lived in a suburb of Nashville, called Madison. My mother was a school teacher. My father was studying to be a Registered Nurse. These are my earliest memories of life. I was 5 when my sister was born. I can picture her lying in her bassinette after my parents brought her home. I remember when we got a TV. I remember watching romper room. I cried when they got a new Timmy on Lassie. One of the children in my mother's school room fell out of a swing and broke her collar bone. I learned a big word clavicle. My father was there when I had my tonsils taken out. He was studying to be a nurse. He obtained his RN license, and then we moved to Duluth, Minnesota. Duluth is the birthplace of Bob Dylan.

My father wanted to become an anesthetist not a Methodist but an anesthetist. An anesthetist is someone who puts you to sleep for surgery. Not an anesthesiologist either. Anesthesiologists are MD's. In Tennessee, they had an 18 month anesthesia program. In Minnesota they had a 12 month anesthesia program. I have always been very proud of my parents for this move. They realized that people are people everywhere. Every place has good and bad people. Another family might not have wanted to move to another state. After all there were Yankees up there. But my parents were not concerned. All my dad knew was that half a year sooner he could be making good money to take care of his family in an affluent manner.

So we went to Duluth. My mother got a job teaching at a Christian school where I would later start the 1st grade. My father registered to start his training at Saint Mary's hospital, in Duluth. He always preferred to drive a Chevrolet over a Ford. But my mother liked Fords. She said she liked the way they handled. So my dad bought a brand new 1957 Ford. Before school started my family took a road trip from Minnesota to see my aunt and uncle in Yakima, Washington. We crossed the

Dakotas, and headed toward the Rockies. We went to Glacier National park. I remember seeing the pictures later on, when I was growing up.

My father had a heavy foot. He was always driving over 70 if not 80 or even 90. Well guess what? The Ford threw a rod through the engine block. My father never owned another Ford. We found ourselves in Chester, Montana. Chester has a population of 847 today. I remember my mother saying that the only paved road in town was the highway that ran through it. More importantly, my mom took me to see Old Yeller. This poignant and sad movie was probably the first movie I ever saw. If you think about it, it might still bring a tear to your eye.

They repaired our car by replacing the engine with an engine from a Rio truck. Did my family turn around and go back to Minnesota? No. We kept going to my aunt and uncles. They owned a farm near Yakima. I guess you would call it a ranch out west. They had dairy cattle, an apple orchard, and they grew hops. I remember my father laughing at me when I was helping to hang up the laundry. One of the women's braziers fell out of the laundry basket. I was too embarrassed to pick it up.

My uncle showed me how he milked the cows. I must have seen that before on farms in Tennessee. I was just too young to remember anything before I came of age so to speak on the Washington trip. While we were there my mom took me to see the movie Thunder Road starring Robert Mitchum. It is a black and white movie about moonshiners in Appalachia. Whenever I have seen this movie on television, I have always noticed the 1957 automobiles.

I remember seeing a newsreel, before the movie started, depicting the Japanese bombing Pearl Harbor. I remember the narrator saying that we must never be caught off guard again. I can still picture seeing the footage of sailors scrambling to their battle stations. The machine guns on board their ship being aimed at the sky, trying desperately to shoot down an attacking Zero. My mother telling me "they could have just kept on coming to California. We couldn't have stopped them." Later in life, I contemplated the logistics of such a thing and realized that it would have been impossible for Japan to move an army from Pearl Harbor to California. But still the point was made. America has always been ready for war ever since that time.

We drove back to Minnesota in our Ford powered by a Rio truck engine. In the summer, I played in a local park. They had ramps there for ski jumping. I climbed up on the things climbing every wrung, as Bob Dylan would say. I couldn't stay forever young however. In the winter, mother took me back there and we watched the ski jumpers gliding down the ramps and soaring into the air. I liked Minnesota. I know it gets quite cold there. I am a California guy. Before California I lived in the south. But when you're 7 you don't mind the cold. The snowmen you build and the snowball fights with other children trump any concerns about a chilly wind.

I remember there was a creek that ran by our school. We used to have great fun throwing rocks into the water, and splashing another kid so that it looked like he had wet his pants. Once I threw a rock into the water and splashed a 6th grader. The slacks he was wearing go wet right in the front, giving him and his pants that look that I spoke of. He got mad, and started picking up big rocks that were almost boulders, causing a giant splash in the creek in an effort to get me back. But it was too late. I ran away, up the hill into the school yard.

My father took me to a hockey game while we were living there. I remember seeing the goalie get hit in the face with a puck. A well struck puck can exceed the speed of a tennis serve or a fast ball. I asked my father, "Why doesn't the goalie wear something like a catcher's mask to protect his face?" My father said, "That's just the way they are." Nowadays of course they do wear a mask to protect their faces. In 1920, Ray Chapman died after being struck in the head by a pitch thrown by Carl Mays. That is the way of the world. It often takes a death or very serious injury before steps are taken to rectify an obviously unsafe situation. How hard was it to see players needed to wear a batting helmet? Poor Carl never got over it.

(9)

Undeclared War

INDO-CHINA

IMAGINE HOW THE people of my father's generation must have felt liberating the Nazi concentration camps. They witnessed such an unimaginable spectacle of horror, suffering, and death. They came home. Some of them became congressmen, some senators, and some of them stayed in the military. Their mind set was that they lived in a world where one nation led by one mad man could try to take over the whole world. The Russians had this mind set too. And America had the bomb and had used it.

Russia distrusted the West. America feared Russia as right we should. Absolute power corrupts absolutely. Russia was a totalitarian state. And Russia is the largest country in the world. Big fish swallow little fish. Factor in China, the most populated country on earth, with the same totalitarian communist ideology and it looked to most of the world like they could be dangerous. The communists, in North Korea, backed by first the Soviets and later by Mao's China, tried to take over the entire Korean Peninsula. In 1954, the French succumbed to the Vietnamese communist at Dien Bien Phu.

My research reveals that approximately 15,700 men were stationed at the French garrison, in northern Viet Nam. 4,500 casualties were sustained by the French, who were supported by the Americans, with 120 cargo planes and 220 fighter aircraft. The United States had 2 pilots killed in action and a few men wounded. The French, having sustained the before mentioned 4,500 casualties, with 1,700 K.I.A., *surrendered the remaining 11,200* soldiers. The Viet Minh, as they were called, allowed the Red Cross to evacuate 800 seriously wounded men. Of the remaining 10,400 only 3,290 came home alive. What a toll! 7,110 died in captivity, about 70%. The Viet Mihn were not nice people. They were ruthlessly pursuing an idealistic goal, with little regard for the toll on human life. These kinds of casualties are deemed unacceptable in the West.

After the French surrender at Dien Bien Phu, the United States of America escalated our involvement in Viet Nam. We orchestrated the dividing of the country through a Geneva agreement. Ho Chi Minh, a communist, ruled North Viet Nam. He drove his army, continually, into the south, in an attempt to reunify the country under his rule. No wonder it seemed to our parent's generation that the communist were trying to take over South East Asia; And that Viet Nam was another Korea, where America needed to make a stand against communist expansion. It seemed that way but this was a misconception. The cost in blood and treasure was disastrous. The horrible destruction America dished out upon the people we were trying to help was appalling.

There is an infamous photo of South Vietnamese General Nguyen Ngoc Loan executing a Viet Cong officer with a single shot to the head. The general later explained that the condemned had recently killed at least 8 people. This accusation is probably true. But prisoners of war are not supposed to be executed after they are captured. We send our sons and daughters to war to fight for freedom and democracy not to support despotic dictators who shoot people without a trial. Isn't that what the contemptuous communist did under Stalin and Mao? Wasn't totalitarianism what we were fighting to save them from?

In 1968, Walter Cronkite publically stated that he believed the war was lost. He said and I quote, "It is increasingly clear to this reporter that the only rational way out then will be to negotiate, not as victors, but as an honorable people who lived up to their pledge to defend democracy, and did the best they could. This is Walter Cronkite. Good night."

In 1973, America withdrew from Viet Nam. In 1975, the North moved their army south, and unified the country. They renamed Saigon Ho Chi Minh City and made it the capital of Viet Nam. With forty  years of hindsight, it seems to me that Viet Nam was not like Korea. The Viet Nam struggle was a civil war between two cultures. One side was Eurocentric and colonial. The other side was Asian and nationalistic.

PERSONAL REFLECTION

My father was in the Navy. He fought in the Battle of the Coral Sea against Imperial Japan. It was the first battle in history where the two opposing navies never saw each other. They each launched their planes from their aircraft carriers. My dad was on the aircraft carrier Lexington, which had been named after Lexington and Concord Massachusetts, the place where the shot heard around the world first rang out.

When Arch Duke Franz Ferdinand was assassinated, in Sarajevo, in 1914, history once again used the slogan "the shot heard around the world." The absolute death of the Divine Right of Kings, in Europe, was accomplished in 1918 at the conclusion of the Great War. After World War I, there was no Kaiser in Germany, no Emperor in Austria, and no Tsar in Russia.

During World War Two the Japanese sank my father's ship the Lexington. He spent the rest of the war going back and forth between Norfolk, Virginia and Casablanca, Morocco. He hunted German submarines, and escorted cargo ships.

I am so proud of my father's service. But, when I was of age, America made a poor decision, becoming involved in a war I couldn't believe in. I did not serve. If any country on the face of the earth should have understood wanting to be rid of a colonial power it should have been the United States of America. As I see it, our fathers liberated the death camps, and saw what a totalitarian regime was capable of. They saw Stalin as another megalomaniac, capable of unspeakable evil; He **was such a man**. Russia is the largest country on earth. China is the most populated country on earth. Big fish swallow little fish. So it is understandable why America feared the Soviet Union and China.

America saved the millions of people living in South Korea from living in what is demonstrably the worst country on the face of the earth. American's laid down their lives defending South Korea from the Communist totalitarians in the north. Did some industrialist get rich from the experience? Of course that is true. But America goes to war in the hope of saving people from deplorable situations. Korea has a population of just over 50,000,000 souls. The United States of America sacrificed 33,000 of her sons in order to save those people from living under the control of the North Korean dictatorship. North Korea is demonstrably the worst place on earth to have to live. Loudspeakers broadcast propaganda into every home. People steal flowers from graveyards to keep from starving.

But Vietnam was a civil war. It was a nationalistic movement and we were Eurocentric in opposing the will of the people to unify their country under the communist Ho Shi Minh. It was misguided, and it was wrong. The American people saw it as another Korea. Korea was not a civil war. It was pure aggression, north against the south. Korea was a test of wills concerning the major powers at the conclusion of World War II. Mankind almost always evaluates the world stage based on the last war, without being able to see a new paradigm developing. This is our history, as I see it, geopolitically.

Now, as then in 1968 when I was sixteen, I ask a moral question too. How could I raise my rifle to my eye and kill a man in Vietnam knowing America was doomed to failure? Wouldn't it be a sin? Thankfully, I never had to go to Vietnam. I know men throughout the ages have fought and died in wars. Picket believed the Confederacy would prevail when he led his famous charge at Gettysburg. So many many battles raged, from Borodino to Waterloo or Dunkirk to Normandy, just to name four. Name any battle in world history, countless thousands have died. They met their maker and went to heaven, whatever that is. My faith teaches me this. I believe this. But kill in a war you know is lost? That was a serious situation to ponder. I believed at the time it was an avoidable sin.

I was blessed with being able to make the choice to say no. I applied for and was granted a conscientious objector deferment. Many applied for this deferment. Many were turned down. But I was not turned down. This great country granted me my deferment. Some young men waited until they had been drafted, and then applied for the deferment. I applied on my 18th birthday. In those days, all males registered for the draft when they were eighteen years old. Then, the draft board selected males to fill the ranks when young men were nineteen. I asked some of my teachers to write letters saying I was sincere. I asked my minister to write such a letter too. I am grateful for their letters. I was sincere.

When I was sixteen, in 1968, I knew Lyndon Johnson was a liar. I knew that he knew all was lost in Vietnam. I had a history teacher who also taught current events. His name was Raymond Haight. He was a great man. He taught us to think objectively, without editorializing about his personal politics. I read the history of Diem

Bien Fu, in 1954, when the French gave up. I read about the logistical support America gave the French at that time. I read about the tactics America tried in vain, to achieve a military victory in Vietnam after the French were gone. All failed. I knew America was not going to win the Vietnam War.

People say America could have won if we had gone all out. That was not the question. The question was, firstly, is America in the right killing all of these people in an undeclared war? For what purpose, I asked? Why to save them from communism of course. The price was often killing everyone in a village because we could not tell friend from foe?

We were in the right in the wars against Germany, and even in Korea. The United Nations voted in favor of the use of force in Korea. But in Vietnam, I think not. Still, does a man have a duty to serve his country? Maybe, and I mean seriously; maybe so. But if a man's country is doomed to failure, then clearly killing another man in a hopeless cause is a major sin. Could America have won that war? The question at the time was not could America win the Vietnam War. The question was **would** America win that war. And the answer was no. I knew we would not. History has proven me correct about this.

America used military force for the greater good in Kuwait and then again in Bosnia, to put a stop to a genocidal civil war. We helped topple Colonel

Kaddafi in Libya too, just to name a few instances of proper usage of military intervention in recent history. America is a great country. Americans are gallant and generous. My only point in writing all of this is our leaders have made some terribly misguided decisions in my lifetime.

What about the Iraq war? Not Afghanistan. Gandhi would have attacked Afghanistan after 9/11. Certainly Al Gore would have. I believe any American President would have responded similarly concerning Afghanistan.

But to link the nation of Iraq to the 9/11 attack in New York City planned by Osama Bin Laden, I believe, never would have been done by any other American President, or any serious candidate for the presidency in American politics be it Kennedy, Nixon, Regan, George Wallace or his running mate Curtis Lemay. Only G.W. *Bush was inclined to make this link. George Bush is an educated man. Yet he led* the American people to a second undeclared war and our clueless congress when along with it.

Concurrently, the Afghanistan situation continued, although it was now de-emphasized in favor of a more concentrated effort in Iraq. Another 150 votes in Florida and none of this would have happened. That travesty of a war in Iraq, followed by the stock market crash in 2008 was all due to George W. Bush and his policies. The invasion of Iraq by the United States of America was Vietnam squared in immorality and disaster.

G.W. decided to cut taxes while we were fighting two undeclared wars and our congress allowed it. All my life I have followed politics. The pendulum swings back and forth most of the time. Tax and spend Democrats come to power and make jobs that fortify our infrastructure. Then Republicans gain power and say those darn liberals are spending us into the poor house. They (Republicans) cut spending and seek to balance the budget by reducing expenditures. This was normal American politics for most of my life. It was normal, and I believe it is good for America. But George W. Bush broke the mold. He exploded deficit spending while lowering taxes. I voted for Barack Obama. In the next election, I plan to vote for Governor Chris Christie. I am an independent voter.

Our sons and daughters went to Iraq, as ordered, and tried to do some good. Americans always do. But to invade and take over a third world country when America or her vital interest had not been attacked, made me ashamed. Iraq might have the bomb they said. Pakistan does have the bomb. Did we invade them? Pakistan was hiding Osama Bin Laden as it turns out. Iraq used to be a country where a man could buy a drink and a woman could get a driver's license. I am not too sure that will be the case after we are gone.

John Kerry voted for the war. Then, ran for president saying it was wrong. Was he confused? Was he a flip flopper? Who knows? He is secretary of State.

Now we have a President who is far from perfect. He picked Kerry to succeed Hilary Clinton. But Obama went on record from the beginning saying the invasion of Iraq should not be coupled with the Afghanistan situation. It looks like Afghanistan is a failed mission now too. But we will never know what might have been the result if we had not diverted our blood and treasure in Iraq.

If anyone reading this served in any of the wars I am talking about, I would salute you if I had ever worn the uniform. I really do regret I was unable to do so in good conscience. When I read about a grown man throwing acid in a little girls face because she is learning how to read, I am ready to get my Winchester and go over there myself even now. And I am sixty three.

Let's hope the baseball diamonds and the soccer fields we are building will do some good. Let us pray that not too many innocent people will be murdered after we are gone.

Maybe the most important point in this discussion of the morality of America's wars since I was born in 1951 is simply this: War is serious business. If America needs to go to war: declare war.

Franklin Roosevelt, U.S. President, during the 2nd World War did declare war. He gave a speech saying

December 7th was a day that would live on in infamy. He said, today a state of war exists between Japan and the United States of America. America has not declared war since 1941. Yet we have gone to war repeatedly.

Our leaders have prosecuted many wars in my lifetime without declaring war. When we were attacked on 9/11, America should have declared war on Afghanistan. If our congress wanted to take over Iraq, they should have declared war on Iraq. Then, once war was declared they should have flattened Fallujah. Understand me. I think waging war against Iraq was a tremendous foreign policy mistake. But if war was going to be waged, we should have declared war. If there were insurgents bent on harming Americans hiding in Fallujah, then Fallujah should have been flattened.

My son had an idea. What is the cost of a cruise missile? The cost is $1,450,000 each. A total of 162 Tomahawk missiles were used in Libya. That is a total cost of $234,900,000. Why not bomb Al-Qaeda and ISIS with our money? Imagine 1,000,000 quarters raining from the sky from 25,000 feet. How far does a silver dollar have to fall to reach terminal velocity? A million silver dollars cost $1,000,000. A million quarters cost $250,000. A million nickels cost $50,000. Wouldn't this be a cost effective way of bombing an enemy in a third world country? The effect would be multi-faceted. First it would kill a lot of people. Remember this is war. It would humiliate them. And it would put money into the hands of the common man. Much better than flying a C-17 over there and dispersing millions of dollars in $20 bills like we did in Iraq. Hey! It is just a thought.

(10)

Batter Up

PE D's, STEROIDS, and other performance enhancing drugs have dominated the sports' pages. I subscribe to the MLB Network, and also I spend many hours watching ESPN. Day after day, I hear analyst bemoaning how so much time is spent discussing this disgusting subject. I would much rather be discussing the Pirates remarkable season after so many years sub-par play. But he just couldn't help himself I guess. An hour long show was devoted to discussing Alex Rodriguez and his alleged use of PED's.

Robert Griffin 3rd is expected to start at quarterback for the Washington Redskins. Mariano Rivera is retiring with the all-time saves record. But A-Rod and his substance abuse allegations dominate the news. We (the public) are forced to hear about it because this is just about all the talking heads will report on. They all bemoan it but none of them will let it go. It is the lead story on my way to work, and it is the lead story on my commute home from work. Even Erin Burnet's CNN news magazine program leads with this story.

Barry Bonds, Roger Clemons, Mark McGuire and so many others are accused of using steroids. These athletes are proving the premise of this book. Sport is war. I could understand it if a man had toiled away his youth in minor league baseball just hoping against hope for a shot at "the show" and he thought this wonder drug could help him hit the curve ball. It would be wrong but, I could understand it. But it is more than this. Even men that are millionaires and seem to have all the privileges that fame and fortune afford these modern day knights of our society seek to gain an unnatural advantage. They want to win so badly that they will risk their health and safety just to get an edge.

Men are crazy. We are so competitive that we will risk humiliation and disgrace to get a competitive edge. But is this anything new? During the 60's I remember hearing allegations of hormone tampering where women took on the characteristics of a man in order to win an Olympic event.

I took my son, James, to Olympic bicycle racing at the Velodrome, in Dominguez Hills, near Los Angeles, in 1984. It was a boring event where two cyclists raced far apart from each other racing solely against the clock. I guess I just picked the wrong event for the two of us. Once in a while someone would get a flat tire, and his opponent would pedal past him. But this was rare. Later we learned that the winner was disqualified. He had pumped an extra pint of blood into his body.

In the eighties, quite a few of my favorite players were accused of using cocaine before taking the field. Were they stoned? Did this give them an edge or did drugs impair their play?

I love baseball. All my life I have sought to memorize certain statistics. 714 is the number of home runs Babe Ruth hit. 60 home runs is the number of home runs Babe Ruth hit in one season. When I was ten, in 1961, Roger Maris hit 61 home runs. But, Roger played more games. In Babe Ruth's day they only played 154 games.

Now we play 162, as Roger Maris did in 1961. They put an asterisk by the record 61 home runs in the record book. It wasn't Roger's fault they play 162 games in modern times. But he did play more games than Ruth did. And if Maris had only played 154 games he would not have hit the 61st home run. Later, Major League Baseball decided to remove the asterisk. A record is a record they decided.

It used to be if a pitcher pitched a complete nine inning game without allowing a hit he was credited with a no hitter whether he was the winning pitcher or not. But 20 years ago or more they decided that if the pitcher did not win the game he would not be credited with a no-hitter in the record books. You could be the losing pitcher in a baseball game where a batter reached base via a walk. He could be balked to second steal 3rd and come home on a passed ball by the catcher.

Another could reach 1st on an error and then advance on a play at 1st base and come all the way around and score on two successive throwing errors. If the team lost the game two to zero the pitcher would have still been credited with a no-hitter in the old days, after all he never allowed a hit, but not anymore. He must be the winning pitcher to be credited with a no-hitter.

Henry Aaron hit 755 home runs during his entire career. Many people feel this is the record. These people disregard Barry Bonds 762 home runs because of steroids. Sammy Sosa shattered the Babe's 60 and Roger Maris's 61 and hit 66 home runs. That same season Mark McGwire hit 70. In Saint Louis they named interstate highway 70 the Mark McGwire Freeway. Could these sacrosanct records have been broken without the use of steroids?

Many are incensed saying Bonds, McGwire, and Sosa should not be allowed to be enshrined in the Hall of Fame. Many others are being questioned. It is ruining our enjoyment of the national pass time. I tend to take a libertarian attitude about this issue. But it does have to stop. Because if these men who are the biggest stars in the game feel a need to abuse these banned substances, what harmful drugs will our country's teenagers ingest in order to be like their sports heroes?

I am convinced that these drugs are being abused in the NFL, the NBA, the NFL, tennis, and golf. Baseball gets more attention because of these numbers I have chronicled here. Baseball lends itself to statistics better than the other sports do. And the game more closely resembles the games played 80 years ago than the other sports do. Tradition means a lot to baseball purist.

(11)

Duluth Revisited

I WENT BACK TO Duluth, Minnesota, just few years ago with my grown son. They have a really neat bridge that spans the entrance to the Harbor Duluth Shares with Superior, Wisconsin. It is a sort of Draw Bridge; but instead of bending in the middle with each side rising like the jaws of a crocodile, the whole bridge is pulled up like an elevator allowing the ships to pass underneath. They have some huge cargo ships sailing those waters. The Great Lakes are really quite remarkable. You have to keep reminding yourself that these are lakes. Because when you are there you feel like you're on the ocean. They all have sandy beaches for sunbathing and building castles in the sand. I remember my mom taking my sister and me to the beach there on the banks of Lake Superior. Sometimes a ship was entering the harbor, and we had to wait until they would raise the bridge, allowing the cars to drive across to the peninsula where the sandy beach awaited us.

It was nice sharing these memories with my son, James, when we visited there. It was the 4th of July. Little children were there with their parents waiting for the fireworks to begin. We were so far north that it was 10:00 o'clock before the sun set enough to start the fireworks show.

The next day, we drove to Port Washington which is just outside of Milwaukee, about 26 miles. We had tickets to see the Brewers and the Cardinals play. We attended two games. My son didn't have the same connection with the Cardinals that I have. I like Prince Fielder. So I was fine with him routing for the Brewers. James mocked me for being so excited about the hot dogs race they have in the 7th inning. When we got inside, experiencing our first race during the 7th inning stretch, we found some fans betting good naturedly on the outcome.

After three days in Wisconsin, we headed to Chicago to fly home to Los Angeles. It is only 90 miles to Chicago and we had a 5:00 o'clock flight. We had time to enter the city from the far north side and see quite a bit of it. We drove past Northwestern University. We stopped and took a lot of pictures everywhere we went. James thought it was comical how often I would stop to take a picture of a church. I was raised Seventh Day Adventist. When I was about 20 I decided that the Good Lord is in all the Churches. This is something I am absolutely certain of. Some churches can be so sectarian. I would not want to belong to such a church. I also decided that a person could pray to the Lord by his or her bed-side without being a member of any particular church. A person doesn't need a building we call a sanctuary or a cathedral to go and visit God. I was not wrong about that.

However around age 40 I started to recognize that this world wasn't going to get any better like some of us believed in the sixties. Good people need to stand up for something. I sought out an ecumenical Christian church and I found one.

In this book, I have attempted to bring the reader a sampling of my political and historical perspective. I would be amiss if I failed to mention my deep devotion to my faith in our Lord Jesus Christ. He created the uni-verse, incarnated His essence, lived with us, laughed with us, cried, died for us, rose from the dead, and sent His Holy Spirit to sustain us with hope through-out our lives. I became a Congregationalist when I was 40. I am 63 now.

William Brewster sailed on the Mayflower in 1620. The descendants of those hardy souls who experienced the first American Thanksgiving formed the Congregational Denomination. The Congregationalists established Harvard University. It is the oldest college in America. I took photos of picturesque churches while on our jour-ney together through the Great Lakes states.

A major theme of my life is a firm belief that the Good Lord is in all the churches. I am currently worship-ping with the Disciples of Christ at the First Christian Church just two miles down the street from my home.

James and I were hoping to stop by somewhere in the neighborhood of Wrigley Field. The Cardinals were playing the Cubs. We had the game on the radio but, we had a plane to catch in three hours. We thought we'd walk around taking pictures, and combine that with a hot dog or a slice of pizza and something to drink. But we could not find any place to park. In all the decades of watching Cubs baseball games on television and listening to people singing the praises of the Wrigley Field experience, no one ever said you better take a bus or a cab if you wanted to get anywhere close to the place. There is no place to park. We were very disappointed.

Chicago is just a different world than what I am used to in southern California. Here we drive everywhere we go. How is a person supposed to frequent the restaurants and sports bars that surround that hallowed shrine if there is no place to park? If the North Side is the "good side" of Chicago, I would hate to see the South Side.

(12)

The Games People Play

THE ANCIENT GREEKS loved competition. Boys and girls are seen playing sports and games on ancient pottery. Young men from the various city states competed against each other in the Olympic Games. Men usually participated in athletic competitions in the nude. It was believed that their gods were pleased by a well-toned body. For this reason women were forbidden from viewing the competition. Of course these games also served the purpose of additional training for soldier. Naturally most of the young men served in the army as warriors. Many of their games were the same competitions we see today in the Olympics Games. Running, jumping, javelin throwing and discus throwing have not changed very much over the millennia. Boys also played checkers, dice, and field hockey. My research reveals that Athenian girls performed acrobatic stunts while clothed where-as in Sparta woman were in the nude. An ancient vase depicts a woman juggling three balls at once fully clothed.

The Isthmian Games were held near Corinth every two years. There were four main events in the Hellenistic times. The most well-known being the Olympics named for Mount Olympus where the gods lived. Saint Paul writes. "Do you not know that in a race all runners run, but only one gets the prize? Run in such a way as to get the prize... They do it to get a crown that will not last; be we do it to get a crown that will last forever. Therefore I do not run like a man running aimlessly" (1 Corinthians 9:24-26 NIV). "A crown that will not last", he says. (1Corinthians 9:25 NIV) He wants humanity to be focused on heaven and re-uniting with the creator. The citizens of Corinth in the 1st Century A.D. were well aware of the importance of sport and we are well aware today.

As I have asserted all along, every sporting event is an attempt to play at war without anybody getting killed. Every board game be it chess or checkers is a war strategy. If it is a game of Monopoly war takes on an abstract connection. The Monopoly game is a financial war between the players. But Stratego is war game like chess. In Stratego you set mines and move your pieces that are labeled captain, sergeant, minor etc. the players attempt to capture the other player's flag. When you play backgammon you attempt to put your pieces into the others player's territory and then pass on over to the other side, so you can take them off the board and win the game. This is similar to a military invasion. In Chinese checkers the goal is very similar. In checkers you reach the other side of the board safely and you earn a crown. You become a king. The game goes on until you have eliminated all your opponent's men. Chess is riveting. The greatest minds in the world grapple for territorial domination until the foe's king is check mated. Eliminating the foe's defending army makes the king more vulnerable. But what makes the cheese more binding in the game of chess as compared to checkers for example is the fact that if you are clever you may be able to check mate the king even though you have a smaller army with which to attack.

When I was in my twenties, my friends and I spent many hours playing war games. War and Peace the board game has a cover depicting the same battle scene that is on my copy of War and Peace, the Tolstoy novel, which is Napoleonic War with Calvary charging into battle. My friends and I loved this game.

Austerlitz is the first scenarios. We played this one the most. It is a recreation of Napoleon's conquest against the Austrian Empire. Austerlitz is in what we used to call Czechoslovakia. It is not too far from Vienna, Austria. Francis the Emperor of Austria allied with Tsar Alexander of Russia suffered a crushing defeat at the hands of the French.

This game came with a very accurate and very detailed map board of Europe. It came in four sections two of which would be about the same size as a Monopoly board. You had little card board pieces called chits. The National Generals are historically accurate with names such as Arch Duke Charles, brother of Austrian Emperor, and Karl Mack for the Austrians, along with the much beloved Russian Prince Bagration killed in battle during the French invasion of Russia. Marshal Kutuzov was the commander of the Imperial Russian Army. But later his death gave way for Count von Bennigsen to lead the Russian army at the Battle of Nation after Napoleon's disastrous frigid retreat from Moscow in the dead of winter. Tsar Alexander joined with the Prussian general Count von Blucher, Francis emperor of Austria, and Prince Charles John of Sweden. Together the four nations defeated the remnants of Napoleon's Grand Army at the Battle of Nations near Leipzig in what is now modern day Germany. Napoleon with Soult, Ney and Messina were noteworthy generals for the French. French general Davout is mentioned in Tolstoy's War and Peace.

Of Course Wellington the British general at Waterloo is included in the game. When battle occurred the dice would determine the out-come. With each roll of the dice the loser would lose a piece. The object was to roll a low number with two dice say a seven for the French and an eight for the Austrian. The French would win that skirmish and the Austrian would lose one of their pieces in the area that was being attacked. What made this game approximate the historical outcome was that when an Austrian Army had a general in his area he could subtract 1. This would turn a roll of six in to a five. (6-1=5). But if Napoleon was at that battle the French would receive a minus three. So if the French rolled a seven their net would be net of four (6-3=4). The modifier with each officer is what made the game fun. And it also made it hard to change history. One of the French allies Bonaparte of Spain was a liability. You see in this game the men cannot move without a general. Bonaparte of Spain would cause his army to have a plus one modifier. So if each adversary rolled ten for example the French would lose (10 + 1 = 11) unless his opponent rolled a 12. Some of the non- French generals had a minus 2 modifier. Most had only a minus one. Wellington of Great Britain had a minus 3 so if you were

playing the battle of Waterloo, the French had no advantage. A few of the French officers were also rated a minus two. Kutuzov had a minus two in the Russian campaign. I simply loved this game. I have one in my home. It was the last one at Amazon.com when I ordered it. It cost me $40. And I will probably never play it again. I just take it out and look at all the soldiers and Generals depicted on the tiny chits and I enjoy studying the map board daydreaming of conquest. Of course Napoleon was an evil man. He didn't care how many people lost their lives for the sake of his egomania. But few if any of the other kings were any more concerned about their people, especially commoners, than Napoleon Bonaparte. Napoleon was just a better general. Because of this he made his contemporary emperors hate him.

My friends seemed to prefer the World War II board games. I owned Panzer Leader and Squad Leader.

Avalon Hill is a board game company that specializes in war games. They make a game called Acquire. This game is a sophisticated game of financial domination. But they are most well-known for the game Axis and Allies. This is a game of World War II scenarios. They also make Battle Cry. This game is based on the American Civil War. Another of my favorites is called Diplomacy. This game has a beautiful map of Europe set historically just prior to World War I (the Great War). I love maps. Some of the games described here have excellent map boards. None are finer than the War and Peace map board. Diplomacy is played without dice. The element of luck has been removed as much as possible. Opponents had to write down their moves and announce them simultaneously. For instance I might write Germany invades France. The French player might write France defends herself. In this case no movement would take place. However, if the German player had an alliance with Italy and the Italian player wrote Italy invades France as well as the German player having so signified. The alliance would take over France because France would not be able to stand alone against two invading armies. In this example the Axis powers of Germany and Italy would put a chip on France that was the same color as their alliance. The only way to defend France would be for the French player to form an alliance through diplomacy (the name of the game) with Great Britain or Spain. If the British player would write England supports France. Now all four armies would bounce back to their countries of origin and no territory would change hands. This game can be played with several participants or it can be played with two players writing the moves for several countries. It is a guessing game. What if England doesn't support France? What if Germany and France believing the British will support France move east and neither attack France. What if Germany

and Italy each attack Austria-Hungry? What if Russia does not support the Austrian Empire? What if Russia is preoccupied with attacking Scandinavia? These are the "what ifs" that I love about this game. It makes for great conversations when four friends come over to spend the day conquering Europe. We were allotted cards from time to time. Some of these cards called for mandatory treaties. I might turn to my friend and say "here sign this". It meant we had a treaty. In this case no matter what other deal that player might have just made with another player, opponent or ally, he could not attack my forces during this upcoming turn. This freed my forces to invade without defending against that other person. Some treaty huh!

Avalon Hill made War and Peace in the 70's and 80's. Now it is a computer game. I like computers but I still prefer board games to computer games. I guess I am old school. I owned Squad Leader and Panzer Leader. I recently found Squad Leader on the internet selling for $100. It was $25 when it was new. Squad leader brought war down to the size of an individual squad. The game used dice. A low roll was most helpful. When your men were fired on they seldom were killed outright. You had to consult a chart. K I A (killed in action) was the result of a very low throw of the dice like three or four or less with two dice. Like War and Peace an officer in the stack would modify the calculation as the dice were thrown. If a player threw a five with a minus one officer in the stack his roll then became a four (5-1=4) if four resulted in a

KIA the game piece was removed from the game. But if a seven was rolled (7-1=6) the unit under attack would not receive a KIA but instead the men would be considered "broken". When the game piece was broken the game piece is turned over. It depicts a soldier lying on his back with his rifle discarded to the side. Players would turn over these units and an officer would attempt to rally the forces by way of using his turn to rally the troops. If several pieces were demoralized an officer could attempt to rally them one piece at a time. Usually a player would have to roll six or less to revitalize his men. We called it a pep talk. An officer could use his modifier to achieve his goal of rallying his men. Most had a minus one modifier. Occasionally a major would be included with a minus two modifier. Some officers had no modifier. Some had a plus one because they were poor officers. These less than charismatic officers were undesirable to have under your command but since it took an officer to rally your broken men you had to have for a roll of five with two dice to rally men under their command. (5+1=6) a six plus one would fail and you would have wasted a turn. There was a special rule for the Russian troops in the Stalingrad scenario. If in an attempt to rally his men a Russian officer rolled box cars (12) the men in question would go berserk. This situation called for the Russian soldiers to discard any cumbersome heavy machine guns. The soldiers only goal was to charge straight at the enemy German soldiers in an attempt to destroy the unit in hand to hand combat. There were rules for hand to hand melees a berserk Russian Infantry could destroy a whole squad of German regulars. Squad leader is so much fun! Maybe when I retire I will buy a game if I can find one. I could spend a three day week-end playing a game with my grown son.

Panzer Leader was on a grander more strategic scale. This game was also great! Describing these Avalon Hill games sure takes me back. I am reminded of how much I enjoy Risk. When I was a teen-ager I came up with a game all my friends enjoyed. I got the idea from Risk another great board game about world conquest. I reasoned that if we were destined to spend countless hours studying the map board we might as well learn a real geography lesson. So we started playing a game I invented called the Map Game. We simply used a map of Europe and measured off our moves with a play-ing card. One card length, two card lengths, and three card lengths; about three card lengths would get you from Berlin to Paris. I came up with a price list for muni-tions and the major cities of the world became supply centers based loosely on population.

This price list of equipment from artillery and tanks to fighter bombers varied with the historical period and the location we would war over. We liked Europe. The War Between the States was fought on a map of the Eastern United States. In this game we allotted infantry men in state capitals based on population. In antebellum America the northern sates outnumbered the southern states by a margin of 3 to 1. In my game I made the

population disparity 5 to 3 to make it possible for the southern player to win the game once in a while.

Yes sport is war. We love to cheer our heroes on. War games are fascinating. But war is not sport. War is terrible and should only be a last resort. If this great nation America that I love so goes to war again, I pray that our leaders will declare war. Declare the objective. Secure it with as little loss of life as possible but fight ruthlessly until the war is over. Then declare peace.

Once I read a book about war games. This book described various games on the market and critiqued them. It was an amusing book. One of the chapters was entitled roll five to sack Constantinople. This was an indication of how difficult it would be to sack Constantinople. A roll of five or less with two dice is un-probable. But it can happen. I like to play craps in Nevada at the casinos.

I hate it when my point is the number five. There is no five in the field and no hard way. These games and more specifically the out-come of the battles in these games are dependent on the roll of the dice. Some games use only one die. Squad leader and Panzer leader were like this. But most use two dice. Risk uses two dice. Diplomacy as is an exception which does not use dice. Stratego and chess do not use dice. But most of these games do. These historical scenario games I am describing use named leaders to modify the dice in order to steer the game toward its' historical outcome.

In War and Peace the object is to roll a low number in the battles. Each roll eliminates a soldier. A high roll and your soldiers are in trouble where-as a low roll should assure victory one piece at a time. A cardboard chit of a soldier represents a company of

men. You might have 10 chits while your opponent might have 15. If an Austrian army is commanded by Charles the Austrian receives a minus 2 modifier. If the Austrian army is commanded by Mack the roll of the dice that represents the battle receives a -1 modifier. This makes the 8 a 7 (8-1=7). If the French General Ney (who is a -1 modifier) is in command and the French roll 8 they also receive a minus one modifier. (8-1=7). The outcome would be a tie and each player would roll again. If Charles rolls that same 8 his modifier makes his roll (8-2=6) in this example the French player would lose a man. Then the two players would roll again. But wait. If Napoleon is in an adjacent hex on the map board he can join the battle on the next roll under certain conditions which are usually easily met with a separate roll of the dice. I say these conditions are usually easily met. But sometimes I have had Ney taking a pounding from Mack, who out-numbered him 3 to 2, only to have Napoleon be unable to join the battle through several rolls of the dice because of bad luck hindering his joining the battle. Being out-numbered 3 to 2 causes you to lose more rapidly too. There are stipulations for this as well. If you think this is complicated you are correct. It is extremely complicated. This is why we liked the game so much. If you are attacking a city the dice are modified. If you are attacking across a river the dice are modified. If you are defending with your back to a river, like Grant at Shiloh, the dice are modified against you. But the basic game revolves around the leader modification. Soldiers being attack by Mack or Ney without a general on the scene receive no modifier. If both player roll 7 the player with an officer will win because of his minus one modifier. Back to my example, if Napoleon joins the battle and takes command you receive -3 modifier. If Napoleon rolls 7, seven is the most likely numbered to be rolled with two dice, (7-3=4) his opponent most roll a 4 (4-1=3) with two dice in order to be victorious against Napoleon. A few of the generals are given minus 2 modifiers. Wellington is given a -3 in the Waterloo scenario.

In life just having the odds in your favor does not assure success. You might wonder how Napoleon could ever lose. Well he might roll 9 followed by 11 followed by 10 followed by 9 again. The Austrian might roll snake eyes followed by four followed by 5 (5-1=4) and so forth. The Austrian might attack Napoleon with his back to the river changing Napoleon's minus three to a minus two only. This rolling of the dice explains how the battles are fought. There is roll after roll until all the men of one army are eliminated in the hex being attacked. A stack of men in an adjacent hex may join in the battle if there is an officer on that hex to order it. For me the enjoyment of this game is moving my armies across the map board. I spend hours and hours studying maps. And this War and Peace map board is the finest representation of 19th century Europe I have ever seen. Panzer Leader has a fine map board depicting

Omaha beach and other inland areas of France but nothing compares to the War and Peace map boards.

When my friends and I played Austerlitz the French army would begin in Strasbourg and march toward Vienna. One strategy was to keep a small force in the Alps in the hopes of diverting some of the French army to protecting the French supply line. If the French attempted to destroy this rear guard action they would have to attack a force in the mountains. The mountain defense would nullify the French officer's advantage even if there was no Austrian officer on the scene. A mountain defense gave the defender a -1 modifier when the dice were rolled.

Still every time I played this game, French or Austrian, Kutuzov and his Russians always made it to Vienna only one or two turns before the bulk of the French army could be aligned for battle. And Napoleon and his mar-shals always overcame the Austrian and Russian alliance at Austerlitz. Even so I would be ready to try to defend Vienna again. After I retire and have more time for a game such as this I will enjoy this game again. It is my favorite of all the historical board games. The Russian winter, Waterloo, and the Iberian Peninsula are all sce-narios included in the War and Peace Game.

An interesting fact I learned boning up for this manu-script, Francis I was Francis II before he became Francis I. How did this happen and why? Well after Francis II lost the battle of Austerlitz Napoleon dismantled the Holy Roman Empire. He created an Italian State. The

Holy Roman Empire had existed since Charles Martel defeated the Moors at the battle of Tours in Southern France in 732 A.D. His grandson Charlemagne was crowned Emperor of the Holy Roman Emperor in 774. This title existed until Napoleon dissolved it in 1805 after the battle of Austerlitz. At this time the crafty although defeated Francis II renamed himself Francis I emperor of the Austrian empire and king of Hungry, Croatia, and Bohemia. These kings of centuries past were all so filled with vanity I find them all contemptible. I was reading a book about the Great War where one German general says to another, "you must remember the Kaiser's bread is always warm and his milk is always cold." Such is the life of a royal personage. Thankfully most of them are only in the history books now. For Franz I, as is his highness's German name, war was merely a sport. When he lost the battle of Austerlitz he only renamed himself. How many tens of thousands laid down their lives in battle defending the Holy Roman Empire from the humanist Bonaparte?

And what of Napoleon himself, why did this ego maniac need conquest? He (Napoleon) brought many positive changes to France. He was a byproduct of the enlightenment. He was egalitarian. Under his rule men and women could live and work as equals. The divine right of kings was scoffed at. After the shot heard around the world in Massachusetts mankind influenced by the enlightenment saw a chance to bring down the hereditary rule of kings and queens. Unfortunately the French Revolution is known to history as a barbarous time of treachery and death inside the nation of France from1787 until 1799. The revolution took various political turns. The monarchs of Europe formed a series of coalitions against the upstart French republic attempting to govern itself without a king. In 1799 Napoleon Bonaparte rose to power as the head of state over all of France. The French revolution was over and the Napoleonic Wars would now begin. Austerlitz was a French victory against the 3rd coalition with the Battle of Nations at Leipzig being France against the 6th coalition in n1813. In between the battles Napoleon proclaimed himself Emperor of France in 1804. He needed no papal authority to be emperor and so he placed the crown on his own head. His only demand of the Pope was that his holiness be there as witness.

The Napoleonic Code of Justice is used in most of the world today. This law proclaimed that all government jobs would be given to the most qualified person regardless of class or social status. The law forbade privileges based on birthright and provided for religious freedom.

I read a book in college about Napoleon's invasion of Russia in 1812. The writer posed the query, why didn't Napoleon free the surfs when he invaded Russia? Did his megalomania go to his head? Or was he keeping the idea as an ace up his sleeve for some future plans? No one will ever know. He was a product of the French

Revolution. He was a believer in egalitarianism yet he did not act to emancipate the surfs. It seems to me that for Bonaparte war had become sport. A game he simply could not resist.

(13)

Final Four

IN 1984 I took my son, James, to see Olympic Field Hockey. The venue was held at East Los Angeles College. We saw Pakistan play India. In preparing to put these ideas to pen I have discovered some information about sport in Pakistan. Pakistan has at least three organized sport leagues where females participate; Football (soccer) Cricket and Field Hockey. I was curious to see if a predominately Moslem country would allow any athletic competition with female athletes. The answer is yes. My son and I saw men's field hockey and Pakistan won the competition. Pakistan won the Gold that year.

In 1947 India was granted independence from Great Britain. It was becoming increasingly clear to thinking men and women in the world that the days of colonies and colonial power should be coming to a close. It became impossible for Great Britain to represent freedom of expression and egalitarian values of fairness while at the same time exploiting other countries militarily.

The 1948 Olympics were held in post war London. One of the stars that captivated people's imagination was a thirty year old sprinter and mother of two dubbed by the media "The Flying Housewife." She won four gold medals.

I remember when my son was twelve; we were anticipating the men's collegiate basketball championship. I really enjoy the drama of the college basketball tournament. The hype on the tube was focused on what a shame it was that Saint John's and Georgetown were not paired against each other in the final four. James and I still talk about this when tournament time rolls around in March. I will say "remember how the so called experts bemoaned the final four pairing when you were twelve?"

"Yes," he replies.

"And what happened James?"

"Villanova beat them both." That was in 1985.

My personal favorite was the year Jim Valvano's Wolf pack defeated Houston. North Carolina State used a slow and methodical approach to defeat the Houston Cougars. The Houston team had future NBA stars Clyde the Glide Drexler and Hakeem Olajuwon. The Cougars were a great team but with determination and great coaching by the now departed Jim Valvano N.C. State won the championship in 1983. Ten years later Valvano lost his fight against cancer in 1993.

Of course the U.C.L.A. Bruins are the greatest collegian basketball team of all time. The UCLA men's basketball program, established in 1920, owns an all-time record 11 Division I NCAA championships. The UCLA Bruins teams coached by John Wooden won 10 national titles in 12 seasons from 1964 to 1975, including 7 straight from 1967 to 1973. UCLA went undefeated a record 4 times, in 1964, 1967, 1972, and 1973. It is an unbelievable record. A record that is unapproachable in my view. Kareem Abdul Jabber, formerly Lou Alcindor, played for John Wooden and so did the big red head Bill Walton. Bill Walton won one tittle while playing center for the Portland Trailblazers. Jabar began his professional career in Milwaukee. Later he became one of the all-time great Lakers. It seems funny to have a team in Los Angeles called the Lakers. But it makes perfect sense when you realize the Lakers moved west from Minnesota. Minnesota is nick named the land of 10,000 lakes. When I was a young man my favorite player was Jerry West. Of course everyone likes Magic Johnson. Magic is the best basketball player of all time in my humble opinion. Magic, a very tall point guard, played center in the play-offs once upon a time.

Basketball has no plot. What does that mean? In American football you have more drama than basketball because of the basic plot structure. Picture 1st and 10 then 2nd and 5 then then 3rd and 1 then forth and inches. Should they go for it? Is a first down in this situation worth the risk? If they take a loss the opposing team is going to get the ball deep in our territory. Is it worth the risk to gain another inch or even a yard? Usually I think not. But there is more to it than that. Because if your team maintains possession you may end up scoring a touchdown with the next sequence of plays; this is what I mean by having a plot.

In baseball you have the count. If the count is no balls and two strikes the batter cannot afford to take another pitch for fear it will be strike three. Often a batter will swing at a very bad pitch because he is afraid to take a called third strike. Conversely if the count is 2 balls and no strikes he knows he is going to get a pretty good pitch to hit because he knows the pitcher does not want to go to 3 balls and no strikes. With a 3 and 0 count the batter knows the pitcher has to throw three strikes in a row. Often the batter will take a pitch right down the middle because he knows the pitcher still has to throw two more strikes without throwing another ball because if the pitcher throws 4 balls the batter can walk to first base. A walk is as good as a single strategically but, not nearly as beautiful as a line drive single to center field. A "frozen rope" is a beautiful thing to behold. But it advances the batter no further than a walk.

Next picture a man on first base and let's say one out. If the manager puts on a hit and run he can start the runner. This means that the base runner on first will take off for 2nd base as the pitch is delivered. This is the same as an attempted steal of 2nd base except that the manager may employ a hit and run with a slow base runner. If the batter can deliver a base hit to the outfield especially if he can deliver a base hit to right field the runner can probably advance an extra base all the way to 3rd base. But this is a bonus. The purpose of the hit and run is to avoid a double play on a ground ball. Ground ball put outs are quite common. But if the manager starts the runner as the pitch is delivered the defenders probably will not have time to force the runner at second and then turn two by forcing the batter running to 1st also. That would be a double play. The hit and run is a defensive measure employed to protect the team at bat from a double play. The risk is that if the batter swings and misses the runner will be forced to try to steal the base. The slower the runner the more likely this maneuver is to backfire on the team at bat if the batter swings and misses. So as the pitcher gets deeper into the count the tension increases. The drama becomes ever changing. With a count of 2 balls and 1 strike the odds are the most tempting for the offensive manager. He and the batter know the pitcher does not want to go to a count of 3 and 1. We have discussed what a predicament this is for the pitcher. So the batter is confident he is going to get a strike to swing at. Conversely, if the count is 1 and 2 the pitcher may waste a pitch high and away. They call it a pitch out. They, the battery, decide on a pitch where in which the catcher can stand up immediately as the pitch is delivered so he can throw out a potential base stealer. The point is every at bat presents a different sub-plot within the game. As the count changes and as the innings roll by the drama of the game intensifies. Baseball has plot.

People enjoy many different things. Some people don't follow sports. Some folks love to play cards. Others like playing tennis and or golf because it is a hobby a person can continue after middle age. Some people drive Chevys while others drive Fords.

By 1890, New Yorkers (Brooklyn was a separate city until it became a borough in 1898) routinely called anyone from Brooklyn a "trolley dodger", due to the vast network of street car lines crisscrossing the borough as people dodged trains to play on the streets. When the second Washington Park burned down early in the 1891 season, the team moved to nearby Eastern Park, which was bordered on two sides by street car tracks. That's when the team was first called the Brooklyn Trolley Dodgers. That was soon shortened to Dodgers. Sportswriters in the early 20th century began referring to the Dodgers as the "Bums", in reference to the team's fans and possibly because of the "street character" nature of Jack Dawkins, the "Artful Dodger" in Charles Dickens' *Oliver Twist*.

Other team names used by the franchise which would finally be called the Dodgers were the Atlantics, Grays, Grooms, the Bridegrooms, the Superbas, and the Robins. All of these nicknames were used by fans and sportswriters to describe the team, but not in any official capacity. The team's legal name was the Brooklyn Base Ball Club. However, the Trolley Dodger nickname was used throughout this period, simultaneously with these other nicknames, by fans and sportswriters of the day. The team did not use the name in any formal sense until 1932, when the word "Dodgers" appeared on jerseys for the team. The "conclusive shift" came in 1933, when both home and road jerseys for the team bore the name "Dodgers." Examples of how the many popularized names of the team were used are available from newspaper articles from the period before 1932. A New York Times article describing a game the Dodgers played in 1916 starts out by referring to how "Jimmy Callahan, pilot of the Pirates, did his best to wreck the hopes the Dodgers have of gaining the National League pennant", but then goes on to comment "the only thing that saved the Superbas from being toppled from first place was that the Phillies lost one of the two games played." What is interesting about the use of these two nicknames is that most baseball statistics sites and baseball historians generally now refer to the pennant-winning 1916 Brooklyn team as the Robins. A 1918 New York Times article does use the nickname Robins in its title "Buccaneers Take Last From Robins", but the subtitle of the article reads "Subdue The Superbas By 11 to 4, Making Series An Even Break."

Another example of the ease of use of the different nicknames is found on the program issued at Ebbets Field for 1920 World Series, which identifies the matchup in the series as "Dodgers vs. Indians", despite the fact that the Robins nickname had been in consistent usage at this point for around six years. The "Robins" nickname was derived from the name of their Hall of Fame manager, Wilbert Robinson, who led the team from 1914 to 1937.

Tom Clancy Sheehan was a Major League pitcher. He spent six years in the major leagues between 1914 and 1926. He played for the Philadelphia Athletics and the New York Yankees of the American League and he played for the Cincinnati Reds and the Pittsburgh Pirates of the National League. The 1915 and 1916 Athletics were one of the worst teams in history. Poor Sheehan only won

Tom Clancy Sheehan

five games over the course of two seasons. He was 4 and 9 in 1915 and 1 and 16 in 1916. However he had a very respectable 3.69 ERA. If this glaring anomaly doesn't point out the value of ERA as opposed to a pitcher's won and lost record, I don't know what does. Overall Tom appeared in 146 major league games. He won 17 and lost 39 with a lifetime ERA of 4.00. He accumulated 169 strike outs. When you see a pitcher with a lot of losses in the major leagues you should stops and consider how many other pitchers wish they were good enough to get the chance to lose a game in the major leagues. At first glance a losing record of 1 and 16 like Tom's in 1916 seems atrocious. But consider why he was the man his manager kept turning to before the start of those seventeen games. If someone on that team had been better the manager would have given him the ball.

In 1960 at age 66 he was promoted the field manager of the San Francisco Giants. He only managed one season and was succeeded by Alvin Dark. Sheehan resumed his duties as a scout for the Giants until his retirement. He lived to be 88.

I was drawn to this story during my research for this book because of his name Tom Clancy Sheehan. Tom Clancy is one of my favorite authors. Tom Clancy and the columnist George Will are each big baseball fans that live in the Chesapeake Bay area. They each have an interest in minor league baseball.

George Will wrote an excellent book about baseball entitled Men at Work. I am paraphrasing here but I recall this example of advice from a pitching coach: When you are pitching always alternate your location. Bring the fast ball in under the hands and then go down low and away. Never establish a predictable pattern but always throw inside and then away. If Mickey Mantle is at the plate throw him high and tight and low and away. If Henry Aaron is at the plate throw it high and tight and low and away. If Willie Mays is at the plate throw him low and away and then high and tight up under the hands. If God is at the plate, of course God will know what is coming, but if you pitch Him high and tight and then low and away He will still make out more often than He gets a hit.

I am quoting from a blog written by Mr. Will himself: "The minor leagues reflect the nation's durable regional differences. South Carolinians, for example, are feisty -- they fired on Fort Sumter from places not far from the Ball Park -- so French fries are still called freedom fries at the ball yard."

Tom Clancy created the fictional character Jack Ryan. He was Tom's alter ego I believe. Jack Ryan is my alter ego too. Who wouldn't want to be a hero like this character? A man who in fiction has saved the queen of England from assassination, helped a Russian Nuclear Sub-marine captain to defect to the west, was instrumental in toppling drug king-pins in Columbia and he thwarted an atomic war between belligerents. Jack Ryan smart, strong, patriotic, a good husband, and a good father too.

These words were penned before the very recent passing of the author Tom Clancy. He will be missed. I am sure those who knew him feel the loss more profoundly than a person like me who is just a fan of good story telling. But my condolences to the family and friends of this fine author, he will be missed.

I feel certain that he would have concurred with the premise: Sport is war. But war is not sport.

(14)

Colt McCoy

COLT MCCOY PLAYED college football for the University of Texas beginning in 2006. He was born in a small town in New Mexico and later went to high school in a small town in Texas. He quarterbacked his team in the Alamo Bowl that year. He completed 2 touchdown passes against Iowa for a NCAA record broken the following year by Oklahoma's Sam Bradford.

In 2007 McCoy played perhaps his worst game against the Kansas State Wildcats. He suffered a concussion in this defeat. Still the Longhorns went to the Holiday Bowl in San Diego against the Arizona State Sun Devils. McCoy won the award for Most Valuable Player in that game.

In 2008 Colt McCoy past Rickie Williams for 2nd all-time in University of Texas history in touchdowns both rushing and passing. McCoy led Texas to victory over Ohio State in the Fiesta Bowl.

At the conclusion of 2009 Colt McCoy was in the Rose Bowl on January 7th,, 2010. The game was hosted by the Pasadena Tournament of Roses association and featured the University of Alabama Crimson Tide against the University of Texas Longhorns. Colt injured his shoulder early in the game. The Crimson Tide won the game. This was the end of Colt McCoy's collegiate career.

This week The NFL draft has been taking place. Teams huddle in their war rooms forming their draft strategies. It's a good idea having a draft in professional sports. It promotes parity. The last place team from the previous season gets to pick first. Last season Andrew Luck was the #1 draft pick in the NFL draft. Andrew Luck led his team right into the playoffs in his rookie campaign. This is very rare. Seldom does a rookie quarterback even start games.

Traditionally rookie quarterbacks sit on the bench and observe. They carry around a clip board and a pencil and they take notes. They might take a few snaps at the end of a blow-out game just for practice but otherwise they must wait until they have gained professional experience a little at a time before being thrown to the lions so to speak in a meaningful game. Last year 2012 was different. The war rooms of the NFL teams were exuberant with anticipation of obtaining what was thought to be one of the best graduating classes of recent years. There were a lot of star players graduating at the so called skilled position. Quarterbacks, running backs, and wide receivers were in abundance. This years' draft did not net a quarterback until Buffalo took Florida State's EJ Manual with the 16th pick overall.

The San Francisco 49ers traded their picks in both the 5th and 7th rounds of the 2013 draft for the Cleveland Browns Colt McCoy and the Browns' 6th round pick. The Browns selected McCoy in the 3rd round of the 2010 draft. He played in eight games as a rookie and started 13 games in 2011 before his season was ended by a concussion. Colt McCoy is twenty six. He has thrown 21 touchdowns in the NFL. He is a prime example of an excellent college player who was able to move on into the professional ranks and achieve a modest level of success. He has earned $4,960,000 in the last four years. "I could live on that" you might say. Of course you would be right. But for this young man and many more like him it was a dream come true to play in the NFL. And financially they should be set. But in the war between NFL owners there is more at stake than trophies and bragging rights. The National Football League generates dollars in the billions. The gladiators that take the field every Saturday in the collegiate arena are the proving grounds for the NFL. No money is invested by the NFL in preparing these young men to do battle in the professional arena. The universities themselves make millions and millions of dollars off of these amateur athletes. Their amateur status is strictly maintained by the NCAA (National Collegiate Athletics Association) which regulates, monitors and if appropriate punishes schools for any rule violation. Some have argued that with all the millions if not billions of dollars the universities make off of college football these players should be paid a salary. But I do not think so. Obtaining a college scholarship to a major university is a pretty good reward for services rendered on the grid iron Saturday afternoon. Combine that with the hopes and dreams of having a professional career and you have college football as we know it today. The millions of dollars in revenue that football gathers can pay for all of the other collegiate sports programs. Water polo doesn't generate much revenue. You could say the same for archery and badminton. I actually enjoy watching curling myself. I wonder what the tickets cost to see it live.

So the NFL has the colleges train their gladiators while paying them nothing and then selects a few candidates to enter the arena of the professional ranks while ponying up a million dollars a year to its' participants many of whom will suffer multiple concussions and a precious few will even be maimed for life but we love watching because it is the closest thing we have to watching an actual battle.

(15)

The Battle on the Ice

ALEXANDER NEVSKY

GENGHIS KHAN CREATED a vast empire. It was the largest the world has ever known. Genghis Khan himself lived from 1206 to 1294. This amazingly large empire stretched from the China Sea to the Baltic Sea. All of Asian Russia was over-run by the "Golden Horde." Then for whatever reason the Great Khan decided to stop his conquest short of short of Novgorod. Legends abound in that part of the world that the Great Khan respected Alexander. One possibility is that Alexander had achieved a distinctive victory against the Swedish army around this time in history. Alexander Nevsky paid a monetary tribute to Genghis Khan. This was another factor. The tribute allowed Alexander to focus his army on other enemies. In 1240 Alexander defeated a Swedish army in the battle of the Neva River. The Nineteen year old Alexander was given the Title Nevsky and has thus been known to History as

Alexander Nevsky. Alexander Nevsky ruled the kingdom of Novgorod. It lies just east of the three modern day nations known to the world as the Baltic States (Estonia, Latvia, and Lithuania). In 1242 the Livonian Knights, a lesser order of the Teutonic Knights sacked the city of Pskov in Russia on the Estonian border. At the southern end of Lake Peipus, a huge lake larger then Rhode Island, a great battle took place "The battle on the Ice." Alexander Nevsky raised an army and met the German Knights on the frozen lake. The Knights were accustomed to having their way in battle. A well-armed and well armored mounted knight on horseback was like a modern day tank in comparison to a foot soldier carrying a sword or a spear. The swiftness of the horse combined with the savagery of the knight's lance and sword was too much for most soldiers. Still Alexander led his foot soldiers onto the frozen lake and surrounded the horsemen one by one pulling them from their steeds and killing them until the remaining German Knights retreated from the field. It is the first time known to history when foot soldier defeated mounted knights in a major battle. With the Teutonic Knights turned away from the west and the Swedish foes turned away from the north, Novgorod could build a relationship with Genghis Khan and his empire to the east. The great Khan was satisfied not to take any more territory. Seldom does a conqueror lose his appetite for more conquest. But this seems to be the case here.

The German people have always tried to portray the Slavic peoples as lesser and inferior peoples compared with the Germans. In the middle ages the Teutonic Knights convinced the Pope in Rome that the Poles were a heathen population and thus in need of reformation by the sword. Poland was a Christian country long before the German speaking people embraced the faith but that didn't stop the Knights from gaining Papal approval for a crusade against the "heathen" Poles. In 1410 the German knights prepared for the Battle of Grunwald or the First Battle of Tannenberg. The Battle of Grunwald is what the victorious Poles and Lithuanians called the site of their victory over the Teutonic Knights in 1410. The Battle of Tannenberg is what the Germans called it and it is what they called it in 1914 when the German army virtually destroyed a Russian army 95,000 Russians troops were captured in the action; an estimated 30,000 were killed or wounded, and of his original 150,000 total, only around 10,000 of Russian men escaped. The Germans suffered fewer than 20,000 casualties and, in addition to prisoners captured over 500 guns. Sixty trains were required to transport captured equipment to Germany.

When Arch Duke Ferdinand was assassinated in Sarajevo another reference to the "Shot Heard around the World" became known to history. This time the pistol shot would ignite the Great War in 1914. It too like Lexington and Concord rang out the death knell of divine right of kings only this time for good. At least as

A Soviet poster

far as Europe was concerned. When the Great War was over there would be no Emperor in Austria, no Kaiser in Germany, and no Tsar in Russia.

I recently saw a documentary filmed shortly before Arch Duke Ferdinand was assassinated. Kaiser Wilhelm told Emperor Franz Josef "The Germans are born to lead and the Slavs are born to serve." This is still typical of the Germanic attitude toward the Slavic people.

The Battle of Grunwald or First Battle of Tannenberg (German: *Schlacht bei Tannenberg*) was fought on 15 July 1410, during the Polish–Lithuanian–Teutonic War. The alliance of Poland and the Lithuania led respectively by King Jogaila and Grand Duke Vytautas decisively defeated the German-Prussian Teutonic Knights, led by Grand Master Ulrich von Jungingen. Most of the Teutonic Knights' leadership were killed or taken prisoner. While defeated, the Teutonic Knights withstood the siege on their own fortress and suffered only minimal territorial losses at the Peace of Thorn in 1411. The Knights never recovered their former power and the financial burden of war reparations caused internal conflicts and an economic downturn in their lands. The battle shifted the balance of power in Eastern Europe and marked the rise of the Polish–Lithuanian union as the dominant political and military force in the region for quite some time.

The battle was one of the largest battles in Medieval Europe and is regarded as the most important victory in the history of Poland, Belarus and Lithuania. It was surrounded by romantic legends and nationalistic propaganda, becoming a larger symbol of struggle against invaders and a source of national pride. During the 20th century, the battle was used in Nazi and Soviet propaganda campaigns. Only in recent decades have historians made progress towards a dispassionate, scholarly assessment of the battle reconciling the previous narratives, which differed widely by nation.

Tannenberg is in Poland and formerly in East Prussia, it was transferred (1945) by the Potsdam Conference to Polish administration. Two important battles were fought there. In the first, fought in 1410 between Tannenberg and the nearby village of Grunwald, Polish and Lithuanian forces under Ladislaus II (Ladislaus Jagiello) halted the eastward expansion of the Teutonic Knights. The second and better-known battle (Aug. 27–30, 1914) occurred during the Great War, later to be renamed World War I. Russian armies under generals Samsonov and Rennenkampf had invaded East Prussia from the south and east, respectively. German strategy was to surround Simonov's forces; 90,000 Russian prisoners were taken, and Samsonov committed suicide. Rennenkampf, whose unwillingness to aid Samsonov greatly facilitated the German victory, was defeated soon afterward in the battle of the Masurian Lakes. The Russian advance into East Prussia, though ill-fated, relieved considerably the German pressure against the West during the first critical weeks of the war. The battle of Tannenberg is a central event in Alexander Solzhenitsyn's novel *August 1914* (1972).

The Ice Bowl

The Ice Bowl comes to mind where the Green Bay Packers did battle against the Dallas Cowboys here in America in Green Bay, Wisconsin in 1967. Unlike the famous Battle on the Ice in 1242 no-one was killed. But it too is legendary in American football lore.

American Football used to be divided into two leagues the American League and the National League much like Major League Baseball was and still is. Later in 1970 the two leagues merged and are now rolled into one National Football League with an American Conference and a National Conference. The two conference champions now play each other in the Super Bowl. This year the San Francisco 49ers battled the Baltimore Ravens. I like to picture the Teutonic Knights riding into battle with deer antlers on their helmets like they might have been during the Battle on the Ice. The Ravens were victorious this year. In 1967 Green Bay held serve on their home-field and defeated the upstart Cowboys. Two legendary coaches were involved in the melee. Tom Landry coached for Dallas Cowboys and Vince Lombardi for the Packers.

Bart Starr was the Packers field general. He finished the first scoring drive with an 8 yard touch- down pass to Boyd Dowler. The packer defense forced a three and out and Bart Starr had the ball again. He soon threw a 46 yard pass to Dowler again and the score was 14 to 0.

Bart Starr

Defensive back Herb Adderly intercepted Don Meredith's pass and returned it 15 yards to the Dallas 32. But after a run for no gain and an incompletion, Cowboys lineman George Andrie sacked Starr for a 10-yard loss, pushing Green Bay out of field goal range. Later Bart Starr lost a fumble while being sacked by Cowboys lineman Willie Townes. Townes. Cowboy George Andrie picked up the loose ball and returned it 7 yards for a touchdown. The Packers were able to keep the Cowboys out of the end-zone for the remainder of the half. But the Cowboys did kick a 21 yard field goal to make the score 14-10. The band from University of Wisconsin was scheduled to perform at half time but with the temperature 17 degrees below zero they were unable to perform. In fact some of the young people had to be taken to the hospital with symptoms of Hypothermia. -17 is the coldest temperature ever recorded for a championship game. Now days the League likes to schedule the Super Bowl in a warm weather city.

In the third quarter, the Cowboys finally managed to get a sustained drive going, moving the ball to the Green Bay 18-yard line. But Packers linebacker Lee Roy Caffey ended the drive by forcing a fumble from Meredith that was recovered by Adderly. Then after a Packers punt, Dallas once again got moving with a drive to the Green Bay-30 yard line. But once again they failed to score as Caffey sacked Meredith for a 9-yard loss on third down and Villanueva's missed a 47-yard field goal attempt.

On the first play of the final quarter, the Cowboys took a 17–14 lead with running back Dan Reeve's 50-yard touchdown pass to wide receiver Lance Rentzel on a halfback option play. Now the Packers had to score to keep the game alive. A field goal would send the game into over-time where-as a touch-down would probably win the game for Green Bay. Bart Starr got his team to a first and goal on the 3 yard line. After two rushing plays only gained 1 yard each the ball was now on the 1 yard line. The time on the game clock said 16 seconds Bart Starr called time out. The temperature on the field was now -20. The running backs were having a hard time getting traction on the icy field. Star conferred with Vince Lombardi. It was 3rd down. If the quarter back rolled out he could have the option to throw a pass which of course would stop the clock if it was incomplete. In this scenario after an incomplete pass the Packers could still attempt an almost sure thing field goal from that distance on 4th down to tie the game and force overtime. Bart Starr was a certain hall of famer when he retired. Everyone expected this to be the call. But Star had been sacked 8 times that day. A sack would allow time to run out also. Still everyone expected this to be the play. When the quarter back rolls out to either side he can always run it himself if he sees an opening. He could even run it out of bounds and stop the clock for a 4th down game tying field goal. Anything but a defensive tackle with the ball carrier still in bounds would be acceptable. A defensive tackle of the ball carrier would mean the end of the game and a Dallas victory. Bart Starr called his own number and ran the ball straight up the middle. Behind center Ken Bowman for 6 points. The extra point was kicked and the final score was Green Bay 21 Dallas 17.

Frank Gifford recounted in his 1993 autobiography *The Whole Ten Yards* that he requested and received permission from CBS producers to go into the losing locker room for on-air post-game interviews—a practice unheard of in that era. Gifford, as a New York Giants player and a broadcaster, already enjoyed a friendship with Meredith, and he approached the quarterback for his thoughts on the game. The exhausted Meredith, in an emotion-choked voice, expressed pride in his teammates' play, and said, in a figurative sense, that he felt the Cowboys did not really lose the game because the effort expended was its own reward. Gifford wrote that the interview attracted considerable attention, and that Meredith's forthcoming and introspective responses played a part in his selection for ABC's Monday Night Football telecasts three years later.

Notice the date on this ticket stub; it is New Year's Eve in 1967. The cost is $10 for a championship game. This game will become a legend. The freezing temperature is more than a footnote to this amazing championship game.

Bart Starr, a quarterback, is one of the most popular players ever to suit up. I remember back in the day reading that Starr received more fan mail than anyone else in Wisconsin except Santa Clause. He is a hall of famer and he was the winning quarter back in the "Ice Bowl".

Dandy Don Meredith would go on to become more famous as a color commentator on Monday Night Football. But he too was a fine quarterback. The Monday night game was a land mark innovation because it brought the public a professional football game on Monday night. This gave the working man and woman something to look forward to after the first day back to the work week.

The three commentators on Monday night football all became famous because of it.

Howard Cosell who would become friends with the great Mohammad Ali was a controversial figure. He was the kind of guy other guys love to hate because he was so opinionated. The thing about know it all's that bugs people is that they are usually right.

Frank Gifford a famous New York Giant quarterback was married to Kathy Lee Gifford. Kathy Lee, now a very successful daytime talk show host and author, is enjoying a wonderful career. I enjoy her television program. I admire her accomplishments. She was once married to a famous football quarterback. I suppose she enjoyed going to the games. She probably stills watches Monday Night football. Yet I ask you, do you think she has a fantasy football team where she competes with other men and women for a Yoohoo shower? Fantasy football and rotisserie baseball are past times enjoyed mostly by men. The ladies are welcome to play. But how many will take me up on it?

(16)

The Sports Fan

Is THE Sports fan a week-end warrior? Are we trying to relive our youth vicariously? Would AYSO Soccer, Pop Warner Football or Little League Baseball bring peace to the Middle East? These questions cannot be answered with certainty but I'm certain it would help. Is the World Cup preferable to a World War? We can say with certainty, absolutely yes.

Are men and women of equal value to society and indeed to God almighty creator of us all? We again say absolutely yes. Are men and women the same? No. Women collect shoes while men collect knives. Women are interested in people and there interaction with other souls. Men are more drawn to games of strategy, statistics and analytical data. Women can do a fine job analyzing data. Women have made great Prime Ministers, Queens, and Tsars. But mothers are care givers predominantly where as men are providers of security. In the ancient world men relied on brute strength more than we do today. But cunning men and women have usually been successful. Women have a primordial desire to seek security over adventure. This is not a selfish thing. Mothers look after their children putting their own safety second to their children. Men sacrifice for their families too. I don't like to generalize because I know every situation is unique unto itself. Still the point must be made. Men enjoy following sports through the media more than women do because sport is war to us. We live and die by our teams vicariously.

Every war ever fought had a unique historical situation of some sort. Still we can see certain trends. Every revolution was driven by some sort of unique premise peculiar to the geography of the region and the culture of the people involved still certain trends are observable seen through the lens of history.

Was the Bolshevik Revolution very different from the French Revolution? Not much. Both saw the elimination and execution of the monarchy in their own particular nation states. Both caused thousands if not millions of innocent people to lose their lives. What of the other civil wars in our lifetimes? Nicaragua, El Salvador, and Cuba all were visited by tremendous loss of life because of idealistic fanatic's hell bent on reforming their societies in order to form a better government than the government they replaced.

Why was the American Revolution so successful? Is it because we Americans wrote the history books in the subsequent years? No. We were successful because we had the ocean to protect us from the colonial power we were resisting. Even more important than this lucky geo-graphic position on the globe is our tradition of written laws. Look around the world. America had a revolution. So did India and Kenya. Was there violence? Yes. But was there whole sale slaughter of the civilian population like in Russia and France. No. The English speaking world has a tradition of written laws dating back to the Magna Charta. When Palestine became Israel there was immediately an organized government in place. They didn't have to invent government they already had a government.

Just as every snowflake is unique so is every athlete. Yet every professional female basketball player is teller than the average woman. Most athletes of either sex and every professional sport are taller than average. But there are exceptions.

Calvin Murphy was a guard for the Houston Rockets from 1970 until 1983. He is 5'9" tall. Nate Robinson also 5' 9" plays for the New York Nicks.

Wataru Misaka was the first Asian NBA player. He played for the University of Utah in 1944 through 1947 when the Utes were NIT champions. He signed an NBA contract in 1947. He was only 5' 7". He played only three games in 1948 before being cut from the team. In 1999 he was inducted into the Utah Sports Hall of Fame.

Anthony Webb known to many as Spuds Webb attended Midland college and North Carolina State University. He was drafted by the Detroit Pistons in 1985 and played in the NBA until 1998. Despite being only 5' 7" is credited with winning a slam dunk contest and achieving 42 inch jump in that contest. He played in 814 games for Detroit, Atlanta, Sacramento, and the Orlando Magic. He scored 8072 points in his career.

Earl Boykins is only 5' 5". He spent most of his career as a point guard for the Denver Nuggets. He scored 32 points in 2004. He currently plays for the Washington Wizards.

THE SHORTEST

The shortest player ever to suit up in the NBA is Tyrone "Muggsy" Bogues. He is 5' 3" tall. His professional career began in 1988 with the then expansion Charlotte Hornets. He played for the Hornets for ten years and was one of their most popular players.

Women have become great golfers like Billy Jean King. They are great skiers like Peekaboo Street. And great tennis players like Chris Evert. The WNBA is a viable professional organization with a television audience; Most of these women are very tall.

There are of course exceptions. During the American Civil War there were women that dressed as men. Women disguised themselves as men for a variety of reasons. Some women wanted to experience the same thing some men desired which is the adventure and supposed glory of surviving a military battle. Some women were quite patriotic as were the men of the time. They simply wanted to do their part in the war effort.

There have been female pirates. Jacquotte Delahaye lived in the 1600s. She is rumored to have been very beautiful. This woman owned her own ship and ruthlessly pirated other vessels on the high seas. She once faked her own death to avoid capture. She dressed in men's clothing and used an alias. Eventually she returned to the high seas and a buccaneer's life. It was at this time she obtained the nick name "back from the dead red".

Anne Die-Le-Veut is an interesting character. Her husband was killed in a bar fight in Haiti by a somewhat infamous buccaneer named Laurens De Graaf. Anne enraged by her husband's murder challenged De Graaf to a duel. The buccaneer was very impressed by the woman's bravery and proposed marriage on the spot. Anne accepted and lived as his common law wife fighting by his side countless times as they pirated other ships in the Caribbean Sea. This was in 1693. Laurens was cut down by a cannon ball during a raid in Jamaica. Anne continued to command the ship and crew and fought tenaciously against the Spanish forces engaging her ship. She was however subdued at this time and taken prisoner to Veracruz, Mexico. Later she was transferred to a prison in Columbia. Anne and Laurens had raided each of these places causing much damage and stealing a lot of loot. Still her fame was so great and because of her female sex she was so interesting to people at the time that Louis the XIV was requested to intervene on her behalf. The monarch did so by writing a letter to the King of Spain. Anne was allowed to go free and was never heard from again.

(17)

The Blue Max

DOG FIGHTS IN the sky that's what I call it. Dozens of kites soaring through the air held only buy a thin cord. The inhabitants of Afghanistan, Pakistan, and India enjoy a competition where in which they engage in aerial combat with their high flying kites. People put a razor blade in the nose and attempt to cut the string of other kites leaving them to fly off into the clouds sometimes never to be seen again. The novel Kite Runner and the movie by the same name takes its' name from this sport.

Having your kite loosed from your grasp and watching it fly away could be disconcerting to be sure but preferable to taking a bullet between the eyes. Losing an expensive kite is also preferable to having your gas tank explode and falling to your death from ten thousand feet. It is a dog fight in the sky not between fighter pilot aces but kite handlers with their feet planted firmly on the ground. The brightly colored kites dip and dive and one by one the other kites are set free and soar into the heavens some never to be seen again until at last only one kite remains flying in the sky. The owner of this kite is the winner. Snoopy vs: the Red Baron was delightful in the funny papers. Our hero, a dog named Snoopy, would sit on top of his dog house donning a pair of aviation glasses and a scarf imagining himself patrolling the skies searching for the Red Baron and hoping to shoot him down doing his part to make the world safe for democracy. As I am picturing this in my mind's eye I also reminisce about watching the movie "The Blue Max" starring George Peppard.

Does anyone recall that 1966 movie about aerial combat during the Great War over the skies of France? The hero was a German fighter pilot striving to make an impression on society by winning the coveted medal known to the Germans as the Blue Max. The Pour le Merite meaning for the merit was originally founded by Frederick the Great in 1740. French was the international language at court in most of 18th century Europe. It is ironic that so many recipients of this German medal received their award for actions in battle in wars

Prussian Order "Pour Le Mérite" (The Blue Max) founded in 1740 by Frederick II.

against France. The nationalistic furor between these two countries had much to do with the terrible wars that plagued Europe in the first half of the twentieth century.

Of course the most famous fighter pilot from the Great War is Baron von Richthofen. His name is greatly romanticized as are most of the stories about World War One fighter pilots. Baron von Richthofen never was awarded the Blue Max. He was awarded a slightly lesser medal, the Blue Max being denied because of some technicality. The Baron's exploits were even memorialized in popular music with a rock and roll song in the 60's that went like this: "Ten, twenty, thirty, forty, fifty, or more - the bloody Red Baron was running up the score. Eighty men died trying to end that spree - of the bloody red baron of Germany." The Baron with his bright red plane shot down eighty allied aircraft. Of course each kill also included the death of another human being. But this was war. It wasn't a game. It wasn't sport.

Before the Great War football, what Americans call soccer, was all the rage in Europe. *Furth* won their first German national title in 1914 under English coach William Townley. They faced a team from Leipzig – the defending champions with three titles to their credit – in the final held on the 31st of May in Magdeburg. A 154-minute-long thriller ended with *Furth* scoring a golden goal (overtime) to secure the title.

Two months later July 28th, 1914 hostilities would begin in Europe between the major powers. The second "shot heard around the world" was the assignation of Arch Duke Ferdinand in Sarajevo by Serbian separatist. The war would be known to history as the Great War or the World War until the Second World War. The bloodshed of this war surpassed anything the world had ever known. World War II surpasses the First World War in depravity, casualties, and destruction. Still it seems to me that the first war was worse. It is because of the senseless tactics applied by the generals on both sides and the close proximity of the opposing armies each armed to the teeth with the most modern automatic weapons of the time. They were separated by a short distance of barren land called "No Man's Land" and each army hid its' soldiers in deep trenches only coming out from time to time to charge into enemy machine guns, mortars, artillery, and rifle fire. Miles and miles of trenches left the opposing forces stalemated for four years with intermittent infantry charges across this barren landscape where a hundred thousand casualties could occur in a single battle. It just seems more awful than even the Second World War. Just the Battle of Verdun in 1916 had 337,000 casualties including 100,000 French killed in action. In 1914 the Battle of the Marne saw 500,000 casualties with the French, English and Germans combined. The Second Battle of the Marne took place in 1918 after the United States had entered the war. The Germans suffered 139,000 killed or wounded. The French suffered 95,165 casualties, the British 16,500, the United States lost 12,000 young men to violent death.

In the Second World war Russia lost 20,000,000 souls to the Germans. We have discussed their casualties at Tannenberg. In Normandy France there is a cemetery. 9,387 soldiers are buried there. In 1966 when Charles De Gaul was the President "over there," France withdrew from NATO. The American Secretary

Americans at Normandy

of State, Dean Rusk was informed and asked to remove all American troops from France "as soon as possible". His reply was "Should we also take the ones that are buried here?" You could have heard a pin drop.

The French were fielding soccer teams and so were the English. In 1914 the Irish National Football Team won the British championship. Some say this was Ireland's greatest achievement in sport ever. Ireland would not be granted her independence from Great Britain until 1921.

As Christmas grew near the first year of the Great War German and English troops began crossing over into no man's land and exchanging friendly greeting with the Germans. They sang Christmas carols too. Then someone kicked out a soccer ball and more of the troops on both sides came out of the trenches and played a football match between the two armies. Here war turned to sport. For a little while just one brief moment of the history of this earth, mankind seamed to realize that war is legalized murder. It is insane to risk your life for a monarch. This is the famous "Christmas Truce" of 1914. Officers had to force their soldiers back to the trenches and to fight on.

What jingoist fervor drives mankind to this insanity? Here were men with rifles setting down their guns and kicking around a soccer ball. In a sane world the Kaiser and or his champion would face off one on one with the President of France winner takes all for Alsace-Lorraine. The emperor of Austria would face off with the Prime Minister of the United Kingdom or his champion. Face off on three penalty kicks with a soccer ball the emperor or his champion guarding the goal while the Prime Minister of the United Kingdom gets three kicks for control of the Balkans. How about a little one on one basketball with the first one to twenty points getting the Ruhr? My best friend and I used to play a lot of hoops. Funny I seldom watch a basketball game unless it is the sweet sixteen or the final four. I much prefer baseball and football these days. But when I was young my friend James who I named my son after used to put the headlights on a basketball court outside near where we each lived and shoot hoops until the battery started to go dead. Then we would start the car and play some more. We played one on one, around the world, and horse. How about if the Kaiser played horse with the Tsar of Russia for Konigsberg? Maybe the United Nations could appoint an impartial referee to oversee a soccer game with eleven athletes from Austria and eleven from Serbia. But no; the rulers of this world prefer might makes right. Sport is sporting. War is not sport. War is legalized murder where the victor obtains possessions of dubious value and the loser loses everything; life itself.

In 1914 The United States of America Foot Ball Association established the first truly national championship competition for American soccer called the National Challenge Cup. The Brooklyn Field Club defeated the Brooklyn Celtics before a crowd of ten thousand people in Pawtucket, Rhode Island.

Before America entered the Great War back in 1914 the Boston Braves won the World Series. Babe Ruth pitched his first professional baseball game for the Baltimore Orioles at the age of nineteen. He would latter sign a contract with the Boston Red Sox. Latter still he would be sold, not traded but sold, like Joseph in the bible by the Red Sox to the New York Yankees. Because Boston Red Sox owner wanted to finance a Broadway play called "No No Nanette." Up in Canada the Toronto Blue shirts won their first Stanley Cup defeating the Victoria Cougars. While also in 1914 the first international Figure Skating Championship was held in New Haven Connecticut.

In 1915 the Boston Red Sox defeated the Philadelphia Phillies four games to one. North of the border the Vancouver Millionaires defeated the Ottawa Senators to win their first Stanley Cup.

In 1916 the Boston Red Sox won the World Series defeating the Brooklyn Dodgers. They defeated the Dodgers four games to one just as they had done with the Phillies. The Montreal Canadians won their first Stanley Cup.

In 1917 The Chicago White Sox defeated the New York Giants four games to two. The Seattle Metropolitans won their first Stanley Cup defeating the Montreal Canadians. The National Hockey League was formed on December 19th, 1917 the first National Hockey League game was played. Evidently they were able to play for the Stanley Cup even before the National Hockey League was formed.

1918 the Boston Red Sox defeated the Chicago Cubs four games to two. Boston will go 86 years without another World Series Championship. That is until 2004 when the Red Sox beat my Cardinals in a four game sweep. Two years later they will sweep the Colorado Rockies too. I was happy to see Boston finally get that monkey of its' back and win a championship. It had been a long time. And poor Bill Buckner was such a fan favorite before he let that ball roll between his legs in 1986. The poor fellow had to move to Montana and hope to find some anonymity. But enough is enough for Boston. In my view they can wait another 86 years I am a National League fan. In 1918 the Cubs used three left handed pitchers to neutralize Babe Ruth. Boston kept Ruth on the Bench in the three games he did not pitch. Ruth pitched brilliantly and George Whiteman stared in the outfield. The Cubs lost and they continue to do so. The Cubs have not played in the World Series in my lifetime. Babe Ruth led the major Leagues with 11 home runs that season. Soon the Yankees would make better use of the Babe. The United States curtailed professional baseball September 2nd in order to accelerate mobilization for war.

World War I was centered in Europe. It began on 28 July 1914 and lasted until 11 November 1918. America entered the war in 1917. It was predominantly called the Great War from its occurrence until the start of World War II which I maintain began in China in 1935. Hostilities between Germany, Italy, and Japan which was termed the Axis Alliance ended in 1945 soon after dropping two atomic bombs on Japan.

After the Second World War the leaders of the world began to see things differently. It was not considered fashionable for powerful European countries to lord over weaker African and Asian Nations. In August of 1945 Indonesian's declared their independence. Insurgent war existed with the Dutch government until Indonesian independence was granted in 1949. Kenya gained independence from Great Britain in 1964. The Belgian Congo gained independence in 1960 and was renamed Zaire and still later renamed Democratic Republic of the Congo. These are a few examples of the independent movements throughout the world of historically modern nation states sometimes referred to as third world countries. The point is people do not want to be ruled by outsiders. People deserve to be able to rule themselves the way Americans do. We Americans have had this privilege ever since the Shot Heard Around the World in 1776. Our rights as Americans are inalienable as we flatly state in our constitution. Nevertheless most of the world saw America as an anomaly, a nice idea for those folks over there across the ocean but not practical for nations with a thousand years of history and traditions. The World Wars changed all of that. In America we Americans took a look at ourselves and said having saved the world for democracy in the First World War; it is time to allow women to vote. Women's suffrage became a reality. After the liberation of the Nazi death camps the world was shocked into realizing that bigotry must end. In America in 1947 a great cultural breakthrough occurred: Jackie Robinson was offered a contract to play mayor league baseball for the Brooklyn Dodgers. Sport would help bridge the gap between black and white in America. Across the Atlantic European nations saw that they could no longer hold entire cultures hostage as vassal states. It is now just unacceptable in the eyes of the world.

In India at 11:57 P.M. August 14th, 1947 Pakistan was created and separated from the rest of India. At 12:02 A.M; just five minutes later, India, as well as Pakistan, was granted the status of an independent dominion of the Crown with total independence being granted in January of 1950. The British government decided before granting independence to India they should separate the people along religious lines. Pakistan has many Hindu's but it is predominately Muslim. India has many Moslems but it is predominately Hindu. Was it a good idea to create Pakistan? East Pakistan and West Pakistan certainly seams ill-conceived. In December 1971 India used her military to sever East Pakistan from West Pakistan. The people of Bangla Desh felt alienated from their brother Muslims in West Pakistan because of the vast distance between them. They wanted to be an independent Nation. India herself is to this day fearful of her Islamic neighbor to the north and now aims missiles with nuclear warheads at Pakistan. Pakistan aims her missiles south toward her former homeland. Each believes the country should be unified under a government administered from their capital. Do they have to nuke each other in order to restore the political order of a unified India? They feel the European British imposed this Pakistan and India situation and of course they did. But aren't they better off living separately? Pakistani people can live in a Muslim dominated country with national religious Holidays to their liking. The people of India can say the same. Why must there be war? What of the disputed territories they each claim? They appear to be significant to their national spirit. Is this territory so important that people must risk their very lives to obtain them? Why not play a game of field Hockey with United Nation referees supervising the competition instead? Let the winner lay claim to the Kashmir. Wouldn't this be better than a nuclear war? I feel certain Mahatma Gandhi would approve of this plan. Pakistan might even agree. But India would not. They would not agree because India is much larger than Pakistan. They have more people, more land, and more resources. So in an all-out war India would surely be victorious. Except Pakistan has an alliance with China. China is the most populous country on earth. India is the second most. So India has an alliance with Russia. Russia is the largest country in area on earth. The plot thickens.

(18)

Final Thoughts

I UNDERSTAND SOME OF the ideas put forth in these pages are just pipe dreams. America will never bomb our enemies with a million silver dollars. Churches will never take up a Sunday school collection called nickels for Fallujah. Kings and dictators will never agree to play a soccer game for Alsace Lorraine. Even presidents and prime ministers of democracies will never agree to play a game of horse for the Kashmir.

Kashmir

However competition between rival gangs in a midnight basketball games can go a long way toward curbing violence in the inner city. A company bowling league can really improve morale for the work force. My friends and I used to play Risk on the week-ends. My roommate always tried to take South America and get the two extra men the rules allowed for that. Another friend, a pretty blonde named Natalie, turned to me one time and said, "Mike you seldom take over a continent but then late in the games you will turn in cards and put 35 men in Mongolia and take over the game." I am proud that my friends see me this way.

Sports can bring a family together. My brother and both of his grown children play fantasy football. When I visited Tennessee a few years ago it was on the heels of Lane Kiffin leaving for southern California and a head coaching job for the USC Trojans. His wife (Kiffin) was quoted as having said she did not like Tennessee. I live in the greater metropolitan Los Angeles area. I live 60 miles east of L.A. in an area known to the locals as the inland empire. California is great but, I wouldn't mind living in Knoxville, Tennessee. Anyway we all went to the big game together. Knoxville has a population of 178,000. The University of Tennessee Stadium holds 106,000 spectators. The average cost of a ticket is $60. That is 6 million dollars in revenue just in ticket sales every home game. My brother Todd and I saw the Oregon Ducks play the Volunteers. The Ducks were too much for Tennessee that night. They were too much for

everyone they played all season until the Auburn Tigers defeated them in January to win the National Championship.

Sport can bring a family together. My family is made up of Seventh Day Adventist, Pentecostals, Baptist, Lutherans, and Congregationalist. Some are Democrats and some are Republicans. But we all hate Lane Kiffin. My family in Tennessee feels this way because he disrespected Tennessee and me because I am a fan of the University of Southern California. And I see a team in need of a coach. Did you see the game against Notre Dame? It was at the end of the 2012 season. The Fighting Irish 22 Trojans 13 was the final score. USC had a rookie quarterback that kept the game pretty close. They ran uninspired plays all four downs on first and goal inside the ten yard line. They had an All-American wide receiver, but they never threw the ball to him. The Trojans had been ranked #1 in the pre-season polls. But they finished the season 7 and 5 and unranked. Then they were humiliated 21-7 in the Sun Bowl in El Paso by another unranked team Georgia Tech who was 7 and 7 before the game with USC. The Trojans had scoffed at their opponent believing the Yellow Jackets were an unworthy adversary with a 50/50 record prior to the game. That was in 2012. This season 2013 after a humiliating loss U.S.C. fired Lane Kiffin.

The night this picture (Shown above) was taken my brother Todd and I saw University of Tennessee play Oregon. Tennessee played them close in the first half but then Oregon Ducks scored 30 unanswered points in the second half. After seeing them (Oregon) live in Knoxville, I was hoping they would win the National championship. USC Trojans were on suspension so I decided to route for another west coast team. It was a game for the ages when Auburn defeated Oregon 22 to 19 in the 2010/2011 BCS National Championship Game at the University of Phoenix Stadium in Glendale, Arizona. In the words of Keith Jackson, the game was a real barn burner. Heisman Trophy winner Cam Newton was just too much for the Oregon Defense that night.

Quarterback Pat Sullivan won the Heisman Trophy in 1971 and the great Bo Jackson is the third person to win a Heisman Trophy attending Auburn University. Bo Jackson is one of the greatest athletes in American sports history. His collegian career coupled with his NFL career was spectacular. It is too bad he injured his hip so badly carrying the ball for the Raiders. He was the first notable player to be a major league baseball star as well as an NFL football star. Brian Jordan played both sports and so did Deon Jackson. All of these men were spectacular. But Bo might have been the greatest athlete of all time had he not gotten injured.

Bo was the MVP of the Sugar Bowl in New Orleans in1983. He was the MVP of the Liberty Bowl in Memphis in 1984; culminating with the Heisman in 1985. He was an all-star in the NFL and a Major League Baseball All Star where he was the All-Star Game MVP in 1989. In his rookie season with the Kansas City Royals in 1987 he hit 22 Home Runs with 53 RBI's and 10 stolen bases. He still can be seen in public playing golf in celebrity golf tournaments for various charities.

In 1985 my son was visiting me when we watched Notre Dame play Boston College. Doug Flutie threw a hail Marry pass into the back of the end zone and Boston College defeated Notre Dame. In church the next day our pastor challenged the congregation to name some things they had to be thankful for. Football on the week-ends someone shouted out. The minister didn't look amused. Then another called out "and thank God for Boston College."

Johnny Manziel of Texas A & M was just a freshman when he won the Heisman Trophy. He created some controversy by signing a few too many autographs to  suit the NCAA rules committee. Players are not allowed to profit from participating in collegian sports. The young man signed autographs willingly without charging for them. Still people could sell their autographed memorabilia and so the NCAA suspended the young man for the first half of the first game against Rice another Texas institution. In the Second half "Johnny Football" threw three touchdown passes. Texas A & M started their season 1 and 0.

The Boston Marathon

As this season's World Series comes to an end I had mixed emotions. I am a lifelong Saint Louis Cardinal fan like my dad. But still when you consider the tragedy that occurred during the running of the Boston Marathon when two deranged young men decided to murder innocent people in Boston on Patriot's Day, I can be happy for the Boston fans. Brook Baldwin of CNN news broadcasting from Atlanta seemed happy for the citizens of Boston. I believe the Red Sox victory was cathartic for all of us just like Mike Piazza's home run was that day in 2001 after 9/11 attack on the twin towers. Apparently Boston has found a new general.

We men spend our whole lives following our favorite teams. My aunt played basketball and my grandmother played hockey. Sports are not just for the male of the species. But the box score is predominately read by men. We scour the pages of the sports page. And scouts in every sport use every means at their disposal be it cyber-metric or just plain first hand observation to gain a competitive edge. It is primordial in mankind to aggressively compete with his brothers for resources and for attention. So in this sense sport is war and without sports there will be more war.

I hope my dad has seen his beloved cardinals win the pennant from heaven. It reminds me of a story of two life-long friends named Josh and Clem. They made a pact with each other to come back from the grave and tell the other if there was baseball in heaven. Well one day the older of the two, Clem, passed away and soon after that his friend was lying in bed listening to the rain on his roof. He heard the wind blow his curtains open and he opened up his eyes and squinted in the darkness.

"Clem is that you he whispered tentatively."

"Yes Josh it's me"

"Have you come to tell me something Clem?"

"Yes Josh my friend I have some good news and some bad news."

"Oh. Well give me the good news first."

"O.K. there is baseball in heaven."

"Oh glory be Clem! Well then what on earth could be the bad news?"

"Sorry Josh but, you're pitching on Friday."

Some of the photos in this book we were taken by me with my own camera and others were captured on the World Wide Web.

Epilogue

MUCH TO OUR chagrin as a species mankind loves war. But the good news is: we have sports and board games to live out our impulses for world conquest vicariously. Weather it is the Olympics, the World Cup, the Super Bowl or in a more abstract way badminton or golf, every game is a substitute for the warrior in us all. Chess and checkers are obvious analogies. But whether it is the game of Risk, after all "everybody wants to rule the world", or Sorry every game is a war. Baseball is just a more abstract analogy then football. But the seriousness in which the sports fan approaches his hobby is intense. I buy several baseball periodicals every spring before the season even begins to bone up on the teams that will soon be in pursuit of the pennant.

In modern times the male of the species does not have to worry about Apaches scalping his loved ones. Attila the Hun won't be raiding my village. We don't hunt dear to put food on the table anymore. We go off to our cubbyholes and make our Excel spread sheets and drive home telling ourselves we are still men. How do we cope? We follow our warrior quarterbacks on

Monday night as they general their teams into enemy territory to capture the flag. This vicarious hero worship is healthy for us. We make war but nobody has to get killed.

Finally sport is war but, war is not sport. Our fathers saved the world from Nazi Germany and Imperial Japan. In my lifetime America has fought in many wars yet every one of them undeclared. The future holds many serious challenges for mankind. Evil doers must be confronted no doubt. Still America must think, and by this I mean Congress, long and hard before committing to war. It isn't a game.

Made in the USA
Columbia, SC
23 July 2021